THE TEN GREATEST TEST TEAMS

TEN GREATEST
TEST TEAMS

Tom Graveney
with Norman Giller

SIDGWICK & JACKSON

LONDON

To JPG, BM and JDT
You be the judges

First published in Great Britain in 1988 by
Sidgwick & Jackson Limited
1 Tavistock Chambers, Bloomsbury Way,
London WC1A 2SG

ISBN 0-283-99529-7 (Hardback)
ISBN 0-283-99753-2 (Paperback)

Typeset and designed by Norman Giller Enterprises, Shoeburyness, Essex
Printed in Great Britain by
St Edmundsbury Press Limited, Bury St Edmunds, Suffolk

Contents

ACKNOWLEDGEMENTS

The authors wish to thank the compilers of the following books which were invaluable in helping them to select *The Ten Greatest Test Teams:*

Wisden Cricketers' Almanack, the 'Bible' of the game; *The Complete Who's Who of Test Cricketers* by Christopher Martin-Jenkins; *The Wisden Book of Test Cricket* by statistical wizard Bill Frindall; Roy Webber's 1952 *Who's Who in World Cricket;* various *Playfair Cricket Annuals;* the magnificent *Barclays World of Cricket* edited by E.W. Swanton and John Woodcock; James Gibb's *Test Cricket Records; The Cricketers' Who's Who* edited by Iain Sproat; *The West Indies* by Tony Cozier; any number of books by our favourite cricket writer, John Arlott; also various issues of *The Cricketer* and *Wisden Cricket Monthly,* two marvellously informative magazines. Thanks also to Michael Giller for his Apple-a-day computer skills, the Associated Press, Sport & General and Press Association picture agencies, and that prince of photographers, Patrick Eagar, for keeping us in the picture. Our gratitude also to David Fuller for his striking jacket design. Most of all, our thanks to YOU for playing the selecting game with us.

Opening Spell
Tom Graveney OBE

This book grew out of a conversation I had following an appearance on *Who's the Greatest?*, the argument-provoking ITV series devised by my co-author Norman Giller. I was on the show as a witness for Garfield Sobers, the all-rounder I have always considered the outstanding cricketer of my lifetime. Sobers had Willie Rushton representing him as an advocate who skilfully and passionately argued that he was the greatest all-rounder in post-war cricket. My fellow witness was that captain marvel of the West Indies, Clive Lloyd. Sobers was matched against English hero Ian Botham, who had David Frost putting the case on his behalf and Mike Gatting and Micky Stewart appearing as witnesses. The 12-strong jury quite rightly came down on the side of Sobers by a convincing 9-3 majority vote.

In the hospitality room afterwards the conversation centred naturally on cricket, and we got to arguing about the merits of various teams. It was Norman who stopped me in full flow with the challenge: 'Don't let's *talk* about it. Let's *write* about it.' And so the idea for selecting *The Ten Greatest Test Teams* was born.

Our first job was to settle on which sides should be considered. We decided to confine the list to ten post-war Test teams that had made the biggest impression on me during my 40 years' association with cricket. That left the field open to some marvellous sides, and you will find in the following pages full breakdowns—the players and their performances—of what I consider the ten top teams since Bradman's magnificent Australian squad of 1948, which just happened to be my baptism year in first-class cricket as a rookie batsman with Gloucestershire.

We look at the great teams of each decade since the war, coming into the 'eighties with searching studies of the outstanding Test sides led by Mike Brearley and Clive Lloyd.You will find that English, Australian and, of course, West Indian Test teams are strongly represented in our final list, and also entering this *Greatest Test Teams* argument is a South African side that would

9

gather a lot of supporters as having been one of the strongest teams in cricket history. Two England teams that just failed to make the final selection were Ray Illingworth's 1970s side and the Mike Gatting team that brought self-respect and confidence back into English cricket with their startling performances in the Tests and one-day internationals 'down under' in Australia on the eventful 1986-87 tour. Illingworth's side, boosted by some marvellous bowling from John Snow, was edged out of the top ten because of a home defeat by India, and Gatting's team dropped out of the picture following their 1-0 defeat in the weather-hit series against Imran Khan's Pakistan in the summer of 1987.

We gave careful consideration to teams from New Zealand, India and Pakistan, but none of them had quite sufficient all-round strength to make the top ten ratings. Imran Khan and Javed Miandad—two gifted players who would stand comparison with the best players of all time—made me think twice about the 1987 Pakistanis, but to be honest they would quite probably have lost the series to Mike Gatting's team but for the rain intervention in the first two Tests. The way we worked on the book was that Norman provided all the statistical facts and figures, leaving me to supply the opinions and gut reactions. In short, the facts of the book are Norman's while the feelings are mine.

For a unique finale to this *Ten Greatest Test Teams* book, Norman arranged for all the relevant data on the featured teams to be fed into a computer. There is a player-by-player breakdown of every team. Following the computer verdict I get the final say as to which team I consider to be number one. We cannot claim that our findings are conclusive, but we believe they will encourage you to play the selecting game. It's fascinating and it's fun.

We know that the final selection could start more arguments than it will settle, but debate and friendly disagreement off the pitch is half the attraction of the great game of cricket. I hope you enjoy *The Ten Greatest Test Teams*...and deciding which teams YOU would choose.

10

THE TEN
GREATEST
TEST TEAMS
1

Don Bradman's Australia, 1948

BACKGROUND

There has rarely, if ever, been a more beautifully balanced squad than that which left the shores of Australia in 1948 to defend the Ashes under the command of Don Bradman, the master batsman who was making his farewell to a game he had electrified with unequalled style and success. Apart from The Don himself, the squad sparkled with talent in every department. New ball partners Ray Lindwall and Keith Miller were approaching the peak of their powers, and in support they had the nip and swing of left-arm fast-medium bowlers Bill Johnston and Ernie Toshack; Ian Johnson was a top-quality purveyor of off-breaks with the flight and cunning to trouble the best batsmen on any pitch that offered him the slightest encouragement; veteran opener Sid Barnes had found an elegant and gifted running mate in left-hander Arthur Morris; Lindsay Hassett was an accomplished batsman with a brilliant tactical brain; and behind the stumps Don Tallon stood comparison with the greatest wicket keepers. It was a team for all seasons, and waiting in the wings for his first Test call was a prodigiously talented young left-handed batsman: Neil Harvey. There was an early indication that this Australian side was

11

something a little bit special when in a warm-up match against Essex at Southend in May they accumulated 721 runs on the first day, and were all out ten minutes before stumps! It was an all-time record one-day score, and a young Cambridge undergraduate by the name of T.E. (Trevor) Bailey was later able to boast jokingly that he was in the only team to dismiss the 1948 Aussie tourists inside one day. Skipper Don Bradman led the run rush with 187 at a rate of 90 runs per hour, and Bill Brown (153), Sam Loxton (120) and deputy wicket keeper Ron Saggers (104) also scored centuries. Bradman and Brown shared an astonishing second wicket partnership during which 219 runs were put on the scoreboard in just 90 minutes. Keith Miller had no appetite for the massacre and deliberately surrendered his wicket to Trevor Bailey without getting a run on the board.

TOM GRAVENEY: 'A few weeks after this run harvest against Essex the Aussies came to Bristol for a match against Gloucestershire with whom I had just started my professional playing career after being demobbed from the Army. I was twelfth man but spent much of the match in the field doing more running about than Roger Bannister. Bradman sat out the match, and deputy skipper Lindsay Hassett instructed opener Arthur Morris to get after that great Gloucester spin bowler Tom Goddard. "Let's discourage the England selectors from picking him for the Tests," he said. Morris, a magnificent left-hander who missed the run feast at Southend, held his own one-man banquet. He scored a century before lunch, a second hundred between lunch and tea and was finally out ten short of his triple ton. Australia declared at 774 for 7 by which time they had destroyed Goddard, who returned nightmare figures of 0-186 before retiring to the pavilion with a sore finger and a broken heart. It was a humiliating experience for one of my all-time favourite players who had been a genius of an off-spin bowler over the previous two decades. It was during that match that I got my first look at Ray Lindwall, and I was immensely impressed. He was the only bowler I saw able to get the ball to lift consistently above stump height on that dormant strip at Bristol. I knew then that the England batsmen were going to be in trouble during the Test series.'

THE OPPOSITION

Led by Yorkshire and former Cambridge University skipper Norman Yardley, England looked a strong side on paper although it was not to prove so on the pitch where it really mattered. They had the 'Terrible Twins' of Middlesex, Denis Compton and Bill

Edrich, fresh from their scorching summer of 1947 when between them they had amassed 30 centuries. Len Hutton and Cyril Washbrook were openers of the highest calibre, Godfrey Evans was a bundle of energy and efficiency behind the stumps, and spin bowlers Jim Laker and Jack Young were potential matchwinners given the right conditions. An obvious weakness was the lack of real pace in the attack but, in Alec Bedser, England had one of the finest of all exponents of swing bowling. The England selectors did not help England's cause by continually disrupting the side as they searched in something approaching panic for a winning combination. They called up no fewer than 21 players during the five-match series.

THE TEST MATCHES
FIRST TEST: Trent Bridge (June 10-15)

England batted first on a wicket made lively and unpredictable by rain. The three-pronged pace attack of Lindwall, Miller and Johnston had England's batsmen in total disarray until Laker and Bedser came together at 74 for 8 and put on 89 to push the total up to 165. Johnston (5-36) was the most successful of the Australian bowlers. Bradman (138) and Hassett (137) built the foundation to an Australian reply of 509 despite stunningly accurate bowling from Jack Young who sent down 11 successive maidens. Lindwall strained a groin and was unable to bowl during a second England innings dominated by Denis Compton who made 184 with a remarkable display of grit and concentration. His innings was spread over three days and it was interrupted nine times by rain, bad light or scheduled intervals. He was finally out when he stumbled on to his wicket avoiding a bouncer from Miller whose intimidating bowling was jeered by the spectators at Nottingham, home county of 1930s bodyline specialists Larwood and Voce. Australia reached the victory target for the loss of Morris and Bradman, who went for a duck caught at backward short leg by Hutton off the bowling of Bedser which was a repeat of his first innings dismissal. **RESULT: Australia (509 and 98-2) beat England (165 and 441) by 8 wickets.**

SECOND TEST: Lord's (June 24-29)

England got off to an inspired start when debutant fast bowler Alec Coxon had Sid Barnes caught for a duck by his Yorkshire team-mate Hutton. Then, with just 17 runs on the board, Australia lost Bradman – for the third time in a row to a backward short leg

13

catch by Hutton off an inswinger from Bedser. But it was the only time that England were in command of a match that was decorated with some classical batting from Morris. He stroked his way to 105 in the first innings and 62 in the second to put Australia on the way to victory by 409 runs. A back injury prevented Keith Miller bowling, but Lindwall (match figures of 8-131) – ably supported by Johnston, Toshack and Ian Johnson – proved too lively for the England batsmen who tamely surrendered to a second innings total of 186 when needing 596 runs to win this 150th match between the two countries. Only Denis Compton (53 in the first innings) reached a half century for England. Barnes (141) made amends for his first innings duck and Bradman powered to 89 runs before falling to Bedser for the fifth consecutive time in Test matches. Miller piled in with 74 runs in the second innings despite his back injury. **RESULT: Australia (350 and 460) beat England (215 and 186) by 409 runs.**

THIRD TEST: Lord's (July 8-13)

Denis Compton was again England's hero in a rain-ruined match. England, having made the astounding decision to drop Hutton, were struggling at 32 for 2 in their first innings when Compton mishooked a lifting ball from Lindwall into his face. He went off for repairs including stitches to a gashed brow. The Middlesex and Arsenal all-rounder returned with the score at 119 for 5 and went on to an unbeaten 145 in an England total of 363. In the closing overs of England's innings Sid Barnes was struck under the ribs by a full-blooded pull-drive by tail-ender Dick Pollard. He tried to resume playing but collapsed at the wicket and spent 10 days in hospital under observation. Australia were disrupted by the loss of their experienced opener and struggled against the new ball bowling by Bedser and Pollard. They were rushed out for 221. Cyril Washbrook produced a succession of superb strokes on his way to an unbeaten 85 as England tried in their second innings to build a winning lead. But skipper Norman Yardley was forced to declare at 174 for 3 when rain washed out play on the fourth day. Jack Young had Ian Johnson caught with his second ball on the final day, but then Morris and Bradman stubbornly remained at the same batting ends for 100 minutes as they saw Australia safely home to a draw. It was the eighth successive Ashes match at Old Trafford to be drawn or abandoned. **RESULT: Match drawn. England 363 and 174 for 3 declared; Australia 221 and 92 for 1.**

FOURTH TEST: Headingley (July 22-27)

England thought they had laid victory foundations at 423 for 2, but lost their last eight first innings wickets for the addition of only 73 more runs. Cyril Washbrook (143), Bill Edrich (111), Len Hutton (81) and stubborn nightwatchman Alec Bedser (79) were the main run compilers. England got their first Test taste of 19-year-old Neil Harvey, who became the first Australian left-hander to score a century in his debut Test against England. He and Keith Miller put on 121 in 95 minutes in a whirlwind fourth wicket stand and the run rate quickened when Sam Loxton joined Harvey (112) at the wicket. Loxton crashed five huge sixes on his way to 93 and then Ray Lindwall contributed 77 to lift the Australian reply to 458. Led by Compton (66), Washbrook (65), Hutton (57), Edrich (54) and an unbeaten knock by Godfrey Evans (47), England hauled themselves into what looked a winning position and Norman Yardley declared their second innings closed at 365 for 8 after five minutes play on the final day. Australia were left facing a victory mountain of 404 runs in 344 minutes on a turning pitch. But the spin combination of Laker and Compton caused few problems. Helped by fumbled catches and missed stumpings, Australia managed to reach the target for the loss of only three wickets. Morris (182) and Bradman (173 not out) put them on the winning road with 301 for the second wicket in only 217 minutes. It was Bradman's nineteenth and final century against England. The Australian skipper deliberately allowed young Harvey to make the winning run, and the fact that he declined to hit the winning boundary himself became especially significant in the final Test at The Oval. **RESULT: Australia (458 and 404 for 3) beat England (496 and 365 for 8 declared) by 7 wickets.**

FIFTH TEST: The Oval (August 14-18)

This match will always be remembered for the humiliation of England's batsmen and the heart-stopping final Test innings of the immortal Bradman. England won the toss and it was all they won over the next five days of painfully one-sided cricket. They found Lindwall (6-20) just about unplayable on a rain-affected pitch, and were hurried out in their first innings in less than two and a half hours for 52. It was their lowest total of the century and their second lowest in all Test cricket. Only opener Hutton offered resistance and was last man out after a fighting contribution of 30. Lindwall destroyed England with a lethal spell of 8.1 overs after lunch during which he snatched five vital wickets for eight runs. By the close of the first day Australia were already 101 ahead for the loss of two wickets. Incredibly, one of those wickets was that of skipper Don Bradman who got a standing ovation as he walked out to the middle in his last Test match. Norman Yardley shook his hand and then called for three cheers from the England players. The Don was visibly moved by the reception and his famous concentration was not as finely tuned as usual as he played forward to a googly from Eric Hollies and was clean bowled second ball for a duck. Four runs would have taken his Test aggregate to 7,000 and his average to exactly 100. Grown statisticians, robbed of writing perfect figures into their books, were close to tears that evening! A solid anchor innings of 196 by Morris – including 16 fours – with solid assistance from Barnes (61) enabled Australia to reach 389. Hollies claimed five wickets for 131 in a marathon stint of 56 overs. Once again, only Hutton (64) kept his head and his wicket while all about him lost theirs as England made a feeble attempt to save a match that was continually interrupted by bad light and rain. Hutton, who was on the field for all but the last 57 minutes of the match, batted for just over four hours with a variety of panicking partners. He was finally caught behind by Tallon off Miller, who sent down an eccentric range of balls before finding the one that broke Hutton's resistance on the ground where ten years earlier he had scored his then world record 364 runs. Compton (39), Edrich (28) and John Dewes (10) were the only other batsmen to reach double figures. England were finally all out for 188 and 149 runs short of making Australia bat again. **RESULT: Australia (389) beat England (52 and 188) by an innings and 149 runs.**

THE CAPTAIN

Don Bradman brought to his captaincy all the powers of concentration, the efficiency and the command that made him the greatest compiler of runs the game of cricket has ever known. He was a shrewd, competitive and – when necessary – merciless captain who led by example. The Don skippered Australia in five Test series between 1936 and 1948 and did not lose one of them. One of his greatest qualities as a Test match captain was the ability to get the best out of his players even when the pressure on them was at its peak. He commanded respect at all times, and his players responded to his totally committed approach to cricket by always giving 100 per cent themselves. Bradman made sure he knew everything about the weaknesses and strengths of all Test batsmen so that he was able to set fields to put maximum pressure on them. He could close a game down and become negative when he considered it in the interests of his team; he was also quick to instruct a positive approach if there was a hint of victory on the horizon. The responsibility of captaincy rarely seemed to anchor his personal performances with the bat and his quite phenomenal Test run-making record is never likely to be surpassed. *Test record:* 52 Tests, 6,996 runs (average: 99.94), 29 centuries, 2 wickets (36.00), 32 catches. Captain in 24 Tests (won 15, lost 3 drew 6).

TOM GRAVENEY: 'Don Bradman was past his peak by the time of the 1948 tour, but he was held in such awe that bowlers were intimidated by his very presence at the wicket. Little wonder when you look at his extraordinary record. In 21 years of first-class cricket he averaged a century once in every three innings that he played. He was not the most exciting and entertaining of batsmen, but was untouchable when it came to efficiency and all-round batting strength. He had a self-confidence that was quite chilling and there was not a bowler he did not feel he could master. There was something of a "Little Dictator" about him at the wicket, and an indication of his legendary run-making skill is that it was considered a failure whenever he missed out on a century. If there was a weakness in his captaincy it was his aloof manner and lack of warmth away from the pitch, which meant he did not get the real affection of his players. But he had their total respect, and that's what really counts. Everything about his batting, apart from an unorthodox grip, was textbook stuff. His footwork was quick, his balance exact, his timing perfect and his shots – particularly on the on-side – powerful and deadly accurate. Along with all his polished batting skills he also had the vital ingredient that you will find in the cocktail that goes to make any great batsman – the ability to give total concentration to the job of scoring the *next* run. Once he had hit the 100 mark he would then set his sights on a double century, and six times during his career he went on to make a triple ton. I had the privilege and joy of bowling to him when England played a Prime Minister's X1 at Canberra during the 1962-63 tour. He had been retired for 14 years but showed that he still had an eye for batting by straight driving me for four. I was absolutely delighted to have the king of batsmen putting me away to the boundary. Brian Statham got him out in the next over. It was a sadly short appearance by one of the Masters, but the fact that all we England players were as excited as schoolchildren just to be on the same ground as The Don is a pointer to his legendary status.'

THE PLAYERS

SIDNEY BARNES
Born : June 5, 1916. *Died* : December 16, 1973
Test record: 13 Tests, 1,072 runs (average: 63.05)
3 centuries, 14 catches.
He was a moody man whose self-opinionated manner did not make him popular with some of his team-mates. But nobody questioned his outstanding ability as an opener of real class. His strength was on the off-side and when in form he was exceptionally difficult to dismiss, as his average 82.25 on the 1948 tour proves. There was a dogged determination about his run-making, and it was never more evident than in the Sydney Test against England in 1946-47 when he and Bradman shared a world-record fifth wicket stand of 405, each man scoring 234 runs. He was given to eccentricity and whacky humour. During one 1948 match he disputed a controversial decision by taking a stray dog to umpire Alec Skelding and saying, 'Now all you want is a white stick!'

ARTHUR MORRIS
Born: January 19, 1922.
Test record: 46 Tests, 3,533 runs (average: 46.48)
12 centuries, 15 catches.
'Affable Arthur' was a regular and reliable left-handed opening batsman for Australia for ten years. There was no better player of spin bowling, and he loved to advance down the wicket and hit straight through the spin. He was, however, suspect against high-class seam bowling and was dismissed 18 times in Test matches by Alec Bedser. On his twenty-ninth birthday, Alec presented him with a coaching book entitled *Better Cricket*. His response came in the following Test when he stroked his way to 206 runs.

LINDSAY HASSETT
Born: August 28, 1913.
Test record: 43 Tests, 3,073 runs (average: 46.56)
10 centuries, 30 catches.
At 5 feet 5 inches, Hassett was small in stature but certainly not in ability. He was a superb all-round batsman who could bat in any position but was most effective in the middle order. In attack or defence he was always graceful, and he continually produced the innings that suited the needs of the team. An outstanding tactician, he became a respected Australian captain despite having to live in Bradman's shadow following The Don's retirement.

18

KEITH MILLER

Born : November 28, 1919.

Test record: 55 Tests, 2,958 runs (average: 36.97)
7 centuries, 170 wickets (average: 22.97), 38 catches.

'Match Winner Miller' was one of the finest all-rounders the game of cricket has ever seen and on a par with Ian Botham as an entertainer. A flamboyant right-handed batsman, he could be deadly as a hostile opening bowler, and his prolific partnership with Ray Lindwall lifted him into the land of legend. He was also an agile fielder. Keith was a great character who believed in drinking his fill from life's cup. He was at his most dangerous when trying to shake off a hangover, or in a hurry to get to the races. He played to entertain the crowds and earned the respect and friendship of colleagues and opponents alike with his cavalier approach. Keith was one in a million both as a man and as a cricketer.

SAM LOXTON

Born : March 29, 1921.

Test record: 12 Tests, 554 runs (average: 36.93)
1 century, 8 wickets (average: 43.62), 7 catches.

Loxton never quite fulfilled his potential in the Test match arena. An aggressive batsman who specialized in hitting sixes, he was also a naggingly accurate fast-medium bowler but was unable to hold down a regular Test place. He appeared in the last three Tests matches of the 1948 series and played a major role in the fourth Test at Headingley where he scored a swashbuckling 93 runs which included five towering sixes. His one and only Test century came in his first match against South Africa in Johannesburg in 1949 and, typically, it was scored in whirlwind fashion – the runs coming in just 135 minutes. Following his retirement he went into politics and became an Australian MP, but still kept a close interest in cricket as a Test selector.

IAN JOHNSON

Born: December 8, 1918.

Test record: 45 Tests, 1,000 runs (average: 18.51)
109 wickets (average: 29.19), 30 catches.

Ian was an exceptionally slow off spinner who was always willing to give the ball plenty of air. Not quite in the class of, say, Jim Laker, he was still good enough to trouble the best batsmen with his deceiving flight. He was an average batsman but excelled himself in Australia's first ever Test in India where his contribution of 73 runs helped steer the Aussies to victory by an innings and five runs. His top Test score was 77 against England at Sydney in 1951 when Australia won by an innings and 13 runs. A fine slip fielder and thoughtful tactician, he succeeded Lindsay Hassett as Australian captain – an appointment that did not find favour with some of his team-mates who wanted Keith Miller as skipper. Australia won seven, lost five and drew five of the 17 matches under Johnson's leadership.

DON TALLON
Born : February 17, 1916. *Died :* September 7, 1984.
Test record: 21 Tests, 394 runs (average: 17.13)
50 catches, 8 stumpings.
Don still has plenty of supporters who consider him the finest of all Australian wicket keepers. He was incredibly quick and agile behind the stumps and had such fast hands that he made his difficult job seem easy. He was also an entertaining middle-order batsman who liked to score runs quickly. A particularly loud and persuasive appealer, he was at his best when keeping to Lindwall and Miller and his safe hands helped make the speed twins an even more deadly combination.

RAY LINDWALL
Born: October 3, 1921.
Test record: 61 Tests, 1,502 runs (average: 21.15)
2 centuries, 228 wickets (average: 23.03), 26 catches.
Ray Lindwall was the Rolls Royce of fast bowlers. He had genuine pace and hostility, and used his lethal bouncer sparingly as a surprise weapon. His yorker was wickedly accurate and he swung the ball both ways. He claimed 27 Test wickets on the 1948 tour, and his 6-20 return in the final Test was a magnificent display of sustained fast bowling at its very best. Ray was also a classy lower-middle order batsman, who could set a scorching run rate or defend stubbornly as circumstances dictated.

BILL JOHNSTON
Born : February 26, 1922.
Test record: 40 Tests, 273 runs (average: 11.37)
160 wickets (average: 23.91), 16 catches.
A likeable but very competitive cricketer, Bill was the unsung hero of the 1948 Australian side. He gave marvellous support to Lindwall and Miller with his stunningly accurate left arm fast-medium bowling and was rewarded with 27 Test wickets. A tall, powerfully built man, he could swing the ball either way and extracted bounce from the most placid of wickets. He was a versatile bowler who would often reduce his pace and turn the ball. His batting was entertaining and earned him the nickame of

'The Arms and Legs Man', due to his comical but often successful windmill swipes at the ball.

ERNIE TOSHACK
Born: December 15, 1914.
Test record: 12 Tests, 73 runs (average: 14.60)
47 wickets (average: 21.04), 4 catches.
Ernie was a left-arm medium pace bowler whose value was as a stock bowler who could bowl just short of a length on leg stump for long spells that frustrated any batsman looking for runs. A recurring knee injury forced a premature retirement but not before he had established himself as a bowler of considerable talent.

THEY ALSO SERVED

BILL BROWN
Born: July 31, 1912.
Test record: 22 Tests, 1,592 runs (average: 46.82)
4 centuries, 14 catches.
He was a cautious, reliable opening batsman and a brilliant fielder who played in the first two Tests of 1948 in the middle order. His peak performances came in pre-war Tests.

NEIL HARVEY
(See Richie Benaud's Australia, 1960-61.)

RON SAGGERS
Born : May 15, 1917. *Died* : March 1987.
Test record: 6 Tests, 30 runs (average: 10)
16 catches, 8 stumpings.
A competent wicket keeper and an accomplished middle-order batsman, Saggers played in the fourth Test at Headingley in 1948 when Don Tallon injured a finger. He was a respected skipper of New South Wales, and briefly succeeded Tallon as first-choice Australian wicket keeper.

DOUG RING
Born : October 14, 1918.
Test record: 13 Tests, 426 runs (average: 22.42)
35 wickets (average: 37.28), 5 catches.
Doug was an adventurous but unpredictable right-arm leg-spinner and a swashbuckling tail-end batsman who played in the fifth Test of 1948. He was an effective bowler on hard Australian pitches, but never quite mastered the bowling conditions in England. He also played in just one Test on the 1953 tour .

THE TOM GRAVENEY ASSESSMENT

It's difficult, impossible even, to find a single weakness in Don Bradman's 1948 Australians. For argument's sake, it could be said that the spin department was not quite world class, but that would be unfair on Ian Johnson who could deceive and trick the best batsmen with his flight. The real strength of the squad lay in the opening attack of Lindwall and Miller and the in-depth array of batting masters.

With the possible exception of recent West Indian teams, there has not been a side with a better new ball combination than Lindwall and Miller. Regardless of conditions and climate, they could always be counted on to give opposition batsmen a torrid time; and if they found a wicket that was conducive to fast bowling, then they became virtually unplayable. A point on which modern batsmen might care to ponder is that in those days the new ball was taken after only 55 overs, so there was nearly always shine there to encourage the quickies. Lindwall and Miller were at their absolute peak for sheer pace in 1948, and had slowed a little by the time I faced them in the 1953 series when Lindwall had probably become even more difficult to play because of a sneaky inswinger that he had added to his armoury. A vital factor on the tour of '48 is that Bill Johnston hit the best form of his career with his lively left-arm deliveries, which took a lot of weight off Lindwall and Miller. They could let loose their fastest balls in short, sharp bursts knowing that they had Bill waiting in support. The batting skills ran all the way down into a tail end that could wag with real vigour. The great Bradman was past his peak but still a brilliant batsman; and the likes of Morris, Barnes, Hassett and the mercurial Miller all plundered plenty of runs off an England attack that in all honesty was sadly lacking both in penetration and genuine speed.

The Bradman team looms large on my memory shelf because I was into my first full season as a County cricketer, and I was in awe of them because they were simply head and shoulders above our England squad of that time. I know my memory is not playing tricks when I say they were in a class of their own. There have been better fielding sides. There may have been better bowling sides. There have been better batting sides, but never a side with such awesome all-round strength and ability. And it is this all-round quality that I will be taking into account when I make my final Top Ten selection for the closing chapter.

John Goddard's West Indies, 1950

THE SQUAD:

Allan Rae (4)	Clyde Walcott (4)	Prior Jones (2)
Jeff Stollmeyer (4)	Bob Christiani (3)	Sonny Ramadhin (4)
Frank Worrell (4)	Gerry Gomez (4)	Alf Valentine (4)
Everton Weekes (4)	John Goddard (4)	Hines Johnson (2)

SCOREBOARD: 4 Tests, 3 victories, 1 defeat

Figures in brackets indicate the number of Test match appearances

---

BACKGROUND

West Indian cricket fans could hardly believe their ears when they heard the squad selected for the first tour of England since 1939, and the first in which the West Indies were awarded five-day Test match status. All their great batting favourites were included, Everton Weekes, Frank Worrell and Clyde Walcott—the phenomenal 'three Ws'—along with consistent runmakers of the calibre of opening partners Allan Rae and Jeffrey Stollmeyer. With a batting line-up like that, getting runs was going to be no problem. But who, the fans wanted to know, were Ramadhin and Valentine? What had they done to justify selection? Few people had the answer. The two raw, twenty-year-old spin bowlers were picked mainly at the instigation of tour skipper John Goddard and his vice-captain Stollmeyer, both of them prepared to gamble that these two unknown, untested youngsters could tease and tame the England batsmen.

Sonny Ramadhin, the first in a long line of East Indians to be chosen for the West Indies, was a stripling of a lad plucked from the Esperance village team in south Trinidad. He had never bowled on any surface but matting and was making his first trip outside Trinidad. It was claimed that he could make the ball turn either way, but few established batsmen had faced him, so there was nobody who could give first-hand evidence of his reputed skills.

Alf Valentine, a gangling, bespectacled Jamaican, was a slow, left-arm bowler who had achieved little in the West Indies to suggest he could outwit England's batsmen. He and the tiny, 5 foot 4 inches Ramadhin had each played only a couple of first-class matches, and when they arrived with the tour party little attention was paid to them by the cricket writers who quite understandably thought they had been brought over just for the experience. By the time the tour and the four-Test series was over Ramadhin-and-Valentine rolled off the tongue as one and had become the best known spin combination in cricket.

TOM GRAVENEY: 'Along with a procession of English batsmen, I have embarrassing memories of coming up against Ramadhin and Valentine for the first time. They had established themselves as household names by the time West Indies arrived at Cheltenham for their match against Gloucestershire in the third week in August, just a couple of days after their crushing victory by an innings over England in the final Test at The Oval. Between them they had taken 59 Test wickets while sending England spinning to a 3-1 series defeat. Their exploits had inspired their celebrating countrymen to fill any cricket ground where they appeared with marvellously joyful calypso music, and one line I recall seemed to be on just about everybody's lips in that summer of 1950 – "Those little pals of mine, Ramadhin and Valentine." Well I found out just what all the fuss was about when I went in to bat for Gloucestershire at a time when I was trying to impress the Test selectors that I deserved an England cap. I was out to prove that had I been playing against West Indies I would have been able to give some backbone to the batting. Suffice to say that I was clean bowled by Ramadhin for 19 in the first innings, one of eight victims that he claimed for just 15 runs. That little so-and-so Sonny baffled me again in the second innings, and I was caught by Stollmeyer for our second-top score of 23. He was on his way to running right through our batting again when the equally tricky Valentine popped up with his magical spin and took the last four wickets for seven runs to seal our defeat. It was then that I knew just why England had been beaten out of sight. Eventually we solved the mysteries of both Ramadhin and Valentine but in that summer of 1950 they got as close as any bowlers can to being just about unplayable.'

THE OPPOSITION

With Denis Compton out of action for much of the season with his infamous knee injury and Len Hutton, Bill Edrich and Alec Bedser sidelined at various times, England found it difficult to get a settled side. Norman Yardley was captain for the first three Tests and was then replaced by Freddie Brown, which added to the lack of continuity. The England selectors leant too heavily on a cluster of inexperienced Cambridge University players, John Dewes, David Sheppard, Doug Insole and Hubert Doggart, all of whom had immense promise but were not ready for Test arena combat away from the friendly Fenners pitch. Ramadhin and Valentine got the selectors as confused as the England batsmen and by the time the four-match series was over they had chopped and changed so many times that 25 players faced the West Indies.

THE TEST MATCHES
FIRST TEST: Old Trafford (June 8-12)

There was no hint of the debacle to come when on a dry, crumbling pitch England clinched a 202-run victory after an hour's play on the fourth day. The match was memorable for a first-innings maiden Test century by England wicket keeper Godfrey Evans, and the remarkable Test debuts of two left-arm leg-break bowlers. Valentine, who had match figures of 13-67 against Lancashire on the same ground a few days earlier, took the first eight England wickets in their first innings and finished with a match analysis of 11 for 204. Bob Berry, Lancashire's left-arm magician, almost matched Valentine in his first Test appearance and his 9 for 116 match figures – supported by the accurate leg breaks of Eric Hollies (8 for 133) – steered England to a win that left West Indies skipper Goddard more than a little angry. He made a public protest about the condition of the pitch, stating that in his opinion it had not been prepared for a five-day Test. Some of the England players quietly made the point that he had not complained at lunch on the first day when England were 88 for 5 and with Len Hutton retired hurt. Only a gallant sixth wicket stand between Trevor Bailey (82 not out) and Godfrey Evans (104) saved a rout. An unusual feature of the match was that wicket keeper Clyde Walcott opened the bowling for West Indies in England's second innings because of an injury to Johnson, with Christiani deputizing behind the stumps. **RESULT: England (312 and 288) beat West Indies (215 and 183) by 202 runs.**

25

SECOND TEST: Lord's (June 24-29)

Ramadhin and Valentine became the calypso kings of cricket as they bowled West Indies to their first ever victory in England, and the fact that it was on the Lord's stage added to the delight of their noisy, friendly followers who held an impromptu carnival out in the middle of the world's most famous ground. Only the Lord's groundstaff were not amused. West Indies were in command from the first day during which Allan Rae (106), Frank Worrell (52) and Everton Weekes (63) laid the foundation for a solid first innings total of 326. Ramadhin (6-66) and Valentine (4-48) spun England out for 151 after Hutton and Washbrook had shared an opening stand of 62 before both getting them-themselves stumped. An immaculate undefeated 168 by Clyde Walcott enabled skipper Goddard to declare the West Indies second innings at 425 for six, leaving his spin twins a day and a half in which to bowl England out. Cyril Washbrook (114) and Gilbert Parkhouse (48) put up stubborn resistance but England finally caved in against stunningly accurate bowling. Ramadhin (5-86) included 43 maidens in his marathon 72-over spell. Valentine (3-79) was just as tantalizingly spot-on with his slow left-arm deliveries and 47 of his 71 overs were maidens. England were finally all out for 274, leaving West Indies celebrating an historic and well-earned victory by 326 runs. **RESULT: West Indies (326 and 425 for 6 dec.) beat England (151 and 274) by 326 runs.**

THIRD TEST: Trent Bridge (July 20-25)

While Ramadhin and Valentine were again the match-winners with 12 wickets between them, it was the batting of Frank Worrell and Everton Weekes that made this a Test to savour. Worrell contributed 261 to a West Indies first innings total of 558 after England had struggled to score a modest 223. It was Worrell the bowler who had given England early problems. His swing and the pace of Hines Johnson accounted for six of England's first innings wickets. But it was Worrell the batsman who was the real hero. He and Weekes (129) shared a whirlwind fourth wicket partnership of 283 in 210 minutes. Alec Bedser gave his usual big-hearted performance and finished with 5 for 127 off 48 overs. England made a gritty attempt to climb the run mountain, with Cyril Washbrook (102) and Reg Simpson (94) sharing a record opening stand between the two countries of 212. Then Gilbert Parkhouse (69) and John Dewes (67) added 106 for the second wicket before Ramadhin and Valentine finally took command. Their bowling this time was as much a marvel of stamina as skill. Valentine bowled a Test record 92 overs for a return of three for 140. Ramadhin toiled through 81.2 overs and was rewarded with five for 135. England, with Godfrey Evans pitching in with a plucky 63, managed to creep up to a respectable 436. Rae and Stollmeyer knocked off the victory runs with an unbeaten opening stand of 103. **RESULT: West Indies (558 and 103 for 0) beat England (223 and 436) by 10 wickets.**

FOURTH TEST: The Oval (August 12-16)

West Indies won the final Test and the series, but it was Len Hutton who won the admiration of everybody who witnessed the match. West Indies batted first and amassed 503 runs thanks largely to centuries by Allan Rae (109) and the remarkable Frank Worrell (138), whose sparkling innings was interrupted by a spell of giddiness that forced his temporary retirement. Recalled veteran spinner Doug Wright (5-141) was England's most successful bowler. It then became Hutton versus the West Indies as the stubborn Yorkshire opener scored an undefeated 202, becoming the first and only player to carry his bat throughout a completed innings against the West Indies. The defiant Hutton batted for 470 minutes and scored 22 fours. Only comeback man Denis Compton looked like giving him the necessary support but England collapsed once he was run out for 44 and they were dismissed for 344. Goddard enforced the follow on, and once Hutton had gone for two in the second innings England's hopes of saving the match went with him. They were spun out for 103, with Valentine (6-39) taking his Test series haul to a West Indies record of 33 wickets. His match return was 10 for 160. Ramadhin (3-38) finished with a total of 26 wickets in the series. **RESULT: West Indies (503) beat England (344 and 103) by an innings and 56 runs.**

THE CAPTAIN

It is often said in cricket that a captain is only as good as his players. John Goddard's experience as West Indies skipper possibly lends weight to that argument. In 1950 when he was able to toss the ball to Ramadhin and Valentine and when he had the batting masters Worrell, Weekes and Walcott in unstoppable form he was hailed as a brilliant captain. Seven years later he was brought out of semi-retirement to lead West Indies on another tour of England. This time Valentine was revealed as a spent force, Ramadhin's magic no longer weaved a spell over the England batsmen and only Worrell of the 'three Ws' was firing at full power. Suddenly Goddard found himself being criticized for his captaincy as the West Indies slumped to a series defeat against a Peter May-inspired England team. A solid left-handed batsman and a useful right-arm medium pace or off-break bowler, Goddard was an influential player for Barbados for a span of more than 20 years. His career-best innings came in 1944 when he contributed 218 not out to a fourth wicket stand of 502 with Frank Worrell for Barbados. His top score in Test cricket was an unbeaten 83 against New Zealand in Christchurch in 1956. In the 1948 Georgetown Test against England, he had his best Test bowling figures of 5 for 31. *Test record:* 27 Tests, 859 runs (average: 30.67), 33 wickets (31.81), 22 catches. Captain in 22 Tests (won 8, lost 7, drew 7).

TOM GRAVENEY: 'My Test experience against John Goddard came during the 1957 tour when he was on the receiving end of some pretty savage criticism for what were a sequence of odd decisions. There was a feeling in the West Indies camp that Frank Worrell should have been made skipper rather than bringing Goddard out of semi-retirement. He did not appear to have a real grasp of things in 1957, but you cannot fault his achievements on the 1950 tour when his leadership was one of the factors that helped establish West Indies as a world power. Mind you, with Ramadhin and Valentine weaving their magic and the 'three Ws' in full flow I reckon just about anybody could have skippered that 1950s' side. All you had to do was make sure you tossed the coin properly.'

THE PLAYERS

ALLAN RAE
Born : September 30, 1922.
Test record: 15 Tests, 1,016 runs (average: 46.16)
4 centuries, 10 catches.
The 1950 series in England was the peak of Allan Rae's Test career. A steady and reliable left-handed opening batsman, he often played the vital role of anchor man while players with greater flair like Weekes, Worrell and Walcott were accumulating the runs. He could also score quickly as he proved on his way to two centuries against England in 1950, showing a perfect mixture of gritty determination and controlled aggession. A successful

London club player, he retired from first-class cricket in 1953 to concentrate on a legal career.

JEFFREY STOLLMEYER
Born : April 11, 1921.
Test record: 32 Tests, 2,159 runs (average: 42.33)
 4 centuries, 13 wickets (average: 39), 20 catches.
He was an elegant and free scoring opening batsman who was always looking to punish loose bowling, particularly on the leg-side. A superb close fielder and competent leg-break bowler, Stollmeyer went on to captain the West Indies from 1951 to 1955, but suffered criticism throughout his reign and was never able to establish himself as a commanding leader. He was a popular cricketer before taking on the responsibility of captaincy and he and Gerry Gomez would often entertain players with their calypso performances at after-match parties.

ROBERT CHRISTIANI
Born : July 19, 1920.
Test record: 22 Tests, 896 runs (average: 26.35)
1 century, 3 wickets (average: 36), 19 catches, 2 stumpings.
Christiani was a talented utility player who could turn his hand to just about every facet of the game. A bespectacled British Guianan, he was an accomplished middle-order batsman who batted with typical West Indian grace and power. He was also a deputy wicket keeper, a fine fielder and an occasional spin bowler. During the 1950 tour he accumulated 1,094 runs at an average 45.58. Christiani kept wicket for a spell in the first Test at Old Trafford when Clyde Walcott opened the bowling after Hines Johnson had pulled a muscle. In his Test debut against England in 1947/8 he missed a century by just one run.

EVERTON WEEKES
Born : February 26, 1925.
Test record: 48 Tests, 4,455 runs (average: 58.61)
15 centuries, 49 catches.
Weekes was the most prolific run getter of the 'three W's'. He continually looked to be on the offensive from the start of his innings and could massacre any attack with a wide array of devastating strokes. A short, stocky man, Weekes used his feet whenever possible and was always to the pitch of the ball. His late cut was his most stunning shot that would more often than not produce a boundary. He was also a fearless hooker and would challenge any bowler to bounce him out. He could defend stubbornly when necessary but it was as an attacking master that

this sporting and enthusiastic character will be best remembered. His consistent scoring earned him the highest possible accolade of being dubbed 'the Bradman of the Caribbean.'

FRANK WORRELL
(see Frank Worrell's West Indies, 1963).

CLYDE WALCOTT
Born : January 17, 1926.
Test record: 44 Tests, 3,798 runs (average: 56.68)
15 centuries, 11 wickets (average: 37.09)
53 catches, 11 stumpings.
Walcott was the power-propelled member of this brilliant trio. He possessed awesome strength and hit the ball exceptionally hard from a crouching stance. At his peak he weighed in at 15 stone and used to put every ounce of his muscular 6 foot 2 inch frame into his strokes. His favourite shots – the straight drive and the cover drive – were just about unstoppable when he middled the ball. He was a competent and reliable wicket keeper and in the early days of his Test career he held his place in the side on the strength of his performances behind the stumps alone. Walcott suffered periods of lost form, and could look very ordinary and clumsy when out of touch. But when at the peak of his power and form there is no question that he was one of the greatest batsmen of all time. To add to his all-round strength, Walcott was also a capable medium-pace bowler and a magnificent slip fielder.

GERRY GOMEZ
Born : October 10, 1919.
Test record: 29 Tests, 1,234 runs (average:30.31)
1 century, 58 wickets (average: 27.41), 18 catches.
He was a consistent all-rounder and an unsung but key member of the side. His best performances came when batting for Trinidad on the easy-paced matting wickets, but he never quite managed to maintain this standard in Tests. His one and only Test century was compiled against India in 1948. Gomez worked hard on his bowling and became a dependable fast-medium frontline bowler. He could swing the ball both ways and was lethal in humid conditions. His finest bowling performance came in the Sydney Test against Australia in 1951-52 when he took 7 for 55 in the first innings and 3 for 58 in the second on a perfect pitch and under a blazing sun, with temperatures in the 100s. A fine close catcher with lightning reflexes, he continued to serve cricket after his retirement as an able administrator who was an authoritative summarizer on radio.

PRIOR JONES
Born : June 6, 1917.
Test record: 9 Tests, 47 runs (average: 5.22)
25 wickets (average: 30.04), 4 catches.
The only weakness in this West Indian side was the absence of a top-class genuine fast bowler. Before the Test series, Prior Jones and Hines Johnson were being tipped as the pace partners to beat England, but the pair were not picked together in the Test matches and so did not make the anticipated impact on the tour. Jones was a strong, determined bowler who was capable of bowling long spells of sustained pace, but he lacked penetration at the highest level. Fielding in the deep was a feature of his game and he used to make spectators gasp with the strength and accuracy of his throwing arm.

HINES JOHNSON
Born : July 17, 1910.
Test record: 3 Tests, 38 runs (average: 9.50)
13 wickets (average: 18.30).
Johnson was a tall, gangling fast bowler who played in two Tests in the 1950 series. He made a startling Test debut against England in Jamaica in 1948 when, at the age of thirty-seven, he took five wickets in each innings. But he was not nearly so effective on English wickets and was overshadowed by spin twins Ramadhin and Valentine. Though capable of making the ball lift, the 6 foot 3 inch Johnson was respected for his sportsmanship and rarely tried to intimidate batsmen with the sort of short-pitch bowling that has become so commonplace in the modern game.

SONNY RAMADHIN
Born: May 1, 1929.
Test record: 43 Tests, 361 runs (average:8.20)
158 wickets (average: 28.98), 9 catches.
The speed of Sonny Ramadhin's rise from obscurity to star status has rarely, if ever, been equalled in any field of sport. An orphan of East Indian parentage, he was unknown even to most West Indian cricket fans when he suddenly emerged – along with Alf Valentine – as the West Indies matchwinner on the 1950 tour of England. Statistics tell their own story of his success on his first trip away from his native Trinidad. He bowled more than 1,000 overs and claimed 135 wickets at an average 14.88. In four Tests he bagged 26 wickets at an average 23.23. England's finest batsmen were baffled and bemused by his carefully camouflaged mixture of right arm off-breaks and leg breaks. He was 'found out' later in his career as batsmen treated him with less respect,

but on that first tour this 5 foot 4 inch tall spinner of magic was a true giant of the game.

ALF VALENTINE
Born : April 29, 1930
Test record: 36 Tests, 141 runs (average: 4.70)
139 wickets (average: 30.32), 13 catches.

Alf Valentine announced his arrival as a star of the cricket stage with 11 wickets in his Test debut against England at Old Trafford in the first Test of the 1950 series. He finished the tour with 33 Test wickets, a West Indies record that stands to this day despite the onslaught of the purveyors of pace. Slim and bespectacled, he was deadly accurate and turned the ball wickedly. He didn't possess the wizardry of Ramadhin but he spun the ball more and together they were the perfect spin combination. Valentine took 123 wickets in all during that memorable tour at an average 17.94. Yet at the start of the tour it looked as if the West Indies selectors had made a mistake in putting their faith in him. He struggled to adjust to English conditions but made a sensational late challenge for a place in the team for the first Test by taking 13 Lancashire wickets for 67. From then on he grew in stature and status and a procession of batsmen found him a conjuror whose tricks they just could not fathom.

THE TOM GRAVENEY ASSESSMENT

In this age of pace, pace and still more pace – particularly from West Indian teams – I get quite nostalgic thinking back to that 1950s side led by John Goddard and featuring those 'two little pals of mine, Ramadhin and Valentine.' They complemented each other so perfectly that they were the ideal spin partners, and what gave them an important advantage is that they arrived in England at the start of the tour with few people – including many West Indians – knowing a thing about them. They truly were secret weapons.

I can still see Ramadhin now on my memory screen, cap planted firmly on his head, sleeves buttoned down to the wrists and gliding in off a short run. You would strain the eyes trying to spot what he was doing with his palm and fingers before releasing the ball, hoping to detect whether he was about to bowl a leg break or an offbreak. But he was so clever at disguising his intentions that invariably not only you but also the wicket keeper – usually Clyde Walcott – failed to read it correctly. Valentine at the other end was easier to read but he really pushed the ball through and could tweak it viciously so that it spun sharply even on docile pitches. In later years, we England batsmen managed to fathom the mysteries of both Ramadhin and Valentine, but on the 1950 tour they were often just about impossible to play against with any certainty.

Of course, the 1950 West Indies were anything but just a two-man team. They had one of the strongest batting line-ups of any Test squad in history. The 'three Ws' were in merciless mood. Walcott and Weekes scored seven centuries each on the tour and Worrell six. Weekes seemed to be almost immoveable once he had got his eye in and he compiled one triple century and four doubles. Openers Allan Rae and Jeffrey Stollmeyer could be counted on to provide a strong foundation on which the middle order could build, and positive proof of their strength in depth is that nine batsmen scored more than 1,000 runs during a tour in which the West Indies won 17 and lost only three of 31 first-class matches. They brought Caribbean sunshine to our cricket grounds and it was a delight to watch them even when on the receiving end of their sheer genius.

Len Hutton's England, 1953

THE SQUAD:

Len Hutton (5)	Peter May (3)	Alec Bedser (5)
Bill Edrich (3)	Trevor Bailey (5)	Tony Lock (2)
Don Kenyon (2)	Willie Watson (5)	Freddie Brown (1)
Reg Simpson (3)	Godfrey Evans (5)	Roy Tattersall (1)
Denis Compton (5)	Jim Laker (3)	Brian Statham (1)
Tom Graveney (5)	Johnny Wardle (3)	Fred Trueman (1)

SCOREBOARD: 5 Tests, 1 victory, 4 draws

Figures in brackets indicate the number of Test match appearances

---

BACKGROUND

There has never been a summer of achievement quite like that of
1953. Anybody who was around in Britain at the time will testify
to the accuracy of that statement. There was the June Coronation
of Queen Elizabeth II, the ascent of Everest by Hillary and
Tenzing, the first Derby victory by new knight Sir Gordon
Richards, the Stanley Matthews Cup Final at Wembley and, of
course, a magnificent Ashes series between England and
Australia. On paper—with the first four Tests drawn—it may
look as if the series was dull and generally inconclusive, but out
on the pitch it was one long story of engrossing, exciting and at
times classical cricket with day after day (and sometimes over
after over) the pendulum of play swinging first towards England,
then to Australia and back again.

Australia had held the Ashes for just a few days short of 19
years, the longest period on record. In the fervent hope of
recapturing them the England selectors put their trust in Len
Hutton, the first professional captain to lead a Test team in
modern times. Hutton responded by moulding a team that
reflected not only his dogged competitive spirit but also his

penchant for perfectionism. There were two players in particular who typified Hutton's approach to the series. Alec Bedser was the heart of the team, bowling marathon spells with flair and determination. Trevor Bailey, meantime, was the backbone of the side and broke the spirit of the Australian bowlers with batting that was more about stubborness than skill. Rarely, if ever, has a Test series so captured the imagination and interest of the nation. There were even complaints from manufacturers that industry was being hit because so many workers were taking time off to tune in to the wireless commentaries and the limited television coverage.

TOM GRAVENEY: 'I was fortunate enough to play in all five Tests in that memorable summer of '53, and while for me personally it was not a particularly successful series I felt it a privilege to be a member of a team that showed what could be achieved with the right attitude and approach. Above all else the game of cricket was the winner that summer. Lindsay Hassett's team played it with typical Aussie grit and determination but never at the expense of good sportsmanship, and many friendships were forged during that tour that last to this day. Cometh the hour cometh the man, and Len Hutton emerged as just the sort of tenacious – bloody-minded even – captain that England needed to get us over the psychological barrier that Don Bradman's Australians had erected with the superiority of their performances against us in 1948. The only thing that Len failed to do well was toss the coin. In five tosses he managed to get beaten every time! I have never known such a build-up to a series. Throughout the winter of 1952-53 the topic of conversation wherever cricketers or cricket followers gathered was the same - "the Australians are coming." The men in those baggy green caps had us all tense and excited with nervous anticipation. I had never played against the Australians in a Test match before but since I was knee-high to a grasshopper (or should I say a cricket?) I had been captured by the magic and mystic of the Ashes contests. We knew that somewhere "down there" Miller and Lindwall were loosening up and overhauling their thunderbolts while we sat in the cold of an English winter waiting and wondering, hoping and praying for victory over the old enemy. It just had to be a series to remember...'

THE OPPOSITION

Lindsay Hassett led an Australian squad that had an interesting mix of youth and experience. Arthur Morris, a by now seasoned Neil Harvey and Hassett himself were the batting masters who had been key members of Bradman's '48 tourists, and the bowling attack again featured that magnificent duo Lindwall and Miller, with Bill Johnston – injury prone throughout the tour – in support. Graeme Hole, Alan Davidson and Richie Benaud were among the new faces who were to become so familiar over the following seasons. With Benaud still raw, the Australians did not have an experienced top-class spinner in the squad and this was to prove significant in a series that got under way at Trent Bridge just nine days after the Coronation celebrations.

THE TEST MATCHES
FIRST TEST: Trent Bridge (June 11-16)

Alec Bedser bowled England to the edge of victory only to suffer the frustration of having all his magnificent work cancelled out by the weather. England finished the third day needing187 to win with nine second innings wickets standing. Then heavy rain washed out play on the Monday and a resumption was not possible until late on the final day, leaving a draw as the disappointing outcome. It was heart-breaking for Bedser, who had produced some of the finest medium-paced bowling ever witnessed at Trent Bridge or, for that matter, in any Test arena. The Surrey twin finished with match figures of 14 wickets for 99 runs. Only legendary Yorkshiremen Wilfred Rhodes and Hedley Verity had claimed more victims –15 wickets apiece – in any of the previous 159 England-Australia encounters. On his way to his 19 wickets Bedser overtook the English record haul of 189 wickets and the previous record holder, eighty-year-old S.F.(Sydney) Barnes, was at Trent Bridge to congratulate him. Lindsay Hassett laid a sound foundation to the Australian first innings with a carefully compiled century, and they looked set for a formidable total at 243 for 4 at lunch on the second day. Then Bedser, with splendid support from Trevor Bailey, took over. He swung the new ball around like a boomerang and the last six wickets tumbled for just six runs during 45 minutes of mystifying mayhem for Australia. Bedser's figures were 7 for 55 off 38.3 overs. Then Ray Lindwall, a yard slower but acres wiser and craftier than in 1948, showed that swing was not the prerogative of Bedser. He took three wickets in eight balls without conceding a run as England collapsed to 92 for 6 before bad light stopped play at the end of a breath-taking second day during which the standard of the fielding had matched the magnificence of the bowling. Between lunch and the early close 12 wickets had fallen for just 98 runs. There was no let up in the see-sawing

36

excitement and drama on the third day when 15 wickets fell for 217 runs. Trevor Bailey staged the first of his stubborn resistance movements when he spent 100 minutes over 10 runs while the enterprising Johnny Wardle (29 not out) knocked off the runs that saved England from having to follow on. Lindwall finished with 5 for 57 off 20.4 overs. Then it became the Bedser show again. His deadly accuracy exposed the Australian batsmen to the perils of panic and they were rushed out for a paltry 123, despite a gritty contribution of 60 by opener Arthur Morris. Bedser's marvellous return was 7 for 44 off 17.2 overs. Roy Tattersall, apart from holding two excellent catches, maintained England's stranglehold with three wickets for 22 in a spell of just five overs. The match was perfectly balanced for a thrilling finish when the rains came. **RESULT: Match drawn. Australia 249 and 123, England 144 and 120 for 1.**

SECOND TEST: Lord's (June 25-30)

This Test will always be remembered for a marathon match-saving stand between Willie Watson and Trevor Bailey on the final day of a game that heaved with incident and individual excellence. Both captains, Hutton and Hassett, made first innings centuries; Tom Graveney (78) and Denis Compton (57) each shared a century stand with Hutton; Alec Bedser became the first England bowler to take 200 Test wickets when he ended an inspired innings by Alan Davidson (76); 42-year-old chairman of selectors Freddie Brown made a one-off Test come-back and celebrated with 4 for 82 in Australia's second innings and a hard-hit 28 in the last 35 minutes of the match; Keith Miller (109) and Arthur Morris (89) added 165 for Australia's second wicket in the second innings; and Ray Lindwall, who claimed 5 for 66 in the first innings, swung the bat for a quick 50 and then dismissed openers Hutton and Don Kenyon to put Australia in a strong position at the end of the fourth day's play. But it was Watson and Bailey who stole the match honours with a remarkable rear-guard action. They came together at 12.42 pm on the final day with England struggling at 73 for 4 and 270 runs from victory. Watson marked his debut against the Australians with a pains-taking 109 in 346 minutes. 'Barnacle' Bailey frustrated and infuriated a battery of Australian bowlers with his dour defensive batting and he scored just 71 runs in 257 minutes while perform-ing a magnificent rescue operation for his country. It was 5.50 pm before they were parted, and then Evans and Brown stifled Australia's push for victory in a thrilling finale. **RESULT: Match drawn. Australia 346 and 368, England 372 and 282 for 7.**

THIRD TEST: Old Trafford (July 9-14)

Rain restricted play to little more than 13 hours in total, yet even in that time the match produced some sensational moments. Neil Harvey (122) and Graeme Hole (66) shared a 177 fourth wicket first innings stand that spanned three days' play against an England attack in which Bedser (5-115) was again the dominant force. Hutton (66) and Compton (45) shared a 94-run stand and then Godfrey Evans (44 not out) and the consistent Bailey (27) put on 60 for the seventh wicket to halt Australian hopes of forcing the follow-on. There was an astonishing collapse by Australia in the last hour, with Wardle (4-7) Laker (2-11) and Bedser (2-14) reducing them to 35 for 8 in just 23 overs. It was the ninth successive match between England and Australia at Old Trafford to be drawn or abandoned, and Manchester was adding to its reputation of being the rain captial of England. **RESULT: Australia 318 and 35 for 8, England 276.**

FOURTH TEST: Headingley (July 23-28)

Trevor Bailey was yet again the unconquerable mountain that stood between Australia and victory. He denied them his wicket for 262 minutes in England's second innings while scoring 38 runs and then he took the ball and bowled with nagging accuracy to a legside field to frustrate Australia's attempts to reach the victory target of 177 runs in 115 minutes. Rain again interrupted the play in a match that was notable for Alec Bedser taking over as world-record wicket taker when he dismissed Gil Langley for his sixth wicket of the first innings and his 217th in Test cricket. England, put into bat, were always struggling from the moment that Ray Lindwall clean bowled Len Hutton for a duck with the second ball of the match. Only Graveney (55) got above a half century as England scraped together 167 runs. A stand of 84 between Neil Harvey (71) and Graeme Hole (53) pushed Australia's reply to a respectable 266. Compton (64) and Edrich (61) produced one of their famous double acts in the second innings before Bailey shored up one end while Jim Laker helped himself to a useful tail-end score of 48. With spinner Tony Lock opening the bowling with Bedser, the Aussies fancied their chances of knocking off the 177 runs needed for victory until Bailey, on the instructions of skipper Hutton, elected to bowl to an unashamedly negative leg side field – a defensive ploy that brought a lot of criticism but which saved the game for England. **RESULT: Match drawn. England 167 and 275, Australia 266 and 147 for 4.**

38

Of the thousands of shots Denis Compton played during his glorious career none are better remembered than his sweep for four at The Oval on August 19 1953. It was the final shot of a memorable series and it clinched an eight wicket victory and brought the Ashes back to England for the first time since 1932-33. England triumphed against the odds because no captain before Len Hutton had ever led a side to victory after losing every toss in a series. England's selectors were rewarded for at last finding a balanced attack. They brought the young tiger Freddie Trueman in to share the new ball with the old warhorse Alec Bedser and had Surrey spin twins Jim Laker and Tony Lock operating together on a turf they knew so well. The turning point of what had been an evenly balanced match – turning being the operative word – came on the afternoon of the third day when Laker and Lock suddenly had Australia reeling in their second innings from 59 for 1 to 85 for 6. Ron Archer and Alan Davidson tried valiantly to dig the Aussies out of the hole into which they had been pushed but once Lock (5-45) had claimed both their wickets England were within sight of a marvellous victory. Australia did not have a spinner in the Lock-Laker class to take advantage of the conditions and England reached their target of 132 runs for the loss of two wickets. Fittingly, it was the 'Terrible Twins' of Middlesex, Compton and Edrich, who were together at the wicket for England when Denis struck the winning boundary off the friendly bowling of Arthur Morris. Alec Bedser ended the series with a record collection of 39 wickets and was quite properly regarded as the 'Man of the Series'. **RESULT: England (306 and 132 for 2) beat Australia (275 and 162) by eight wickets.**

THE CAPTAIN

Len Hutton's captaincy was just like his batting – dogged, determined, at times inspired and always, always wrapped in total concentration. He was a master tactician who leant towards caution, but he could encourage a spirit of adventure when the situation called for it. His professionalism showed in everything he did. He laid the foundation to his marvellously successful career with the Pudsey St Lawrence village team before joining Yorkshire after impressing in a trial at Headingley at the age of fifteen. A protege of another Yorkshire opening master, Herbert Sutcliffe, he came under the influence of the great George Hirst whose expert coaching helped shape Hutton into a complete batsman. He perfected a batting technique that was defensive in its concept, enabling him to counter almost any problem posed by the bowler facing him. He became basically a back-foot player and supreme at killing the turning and lifting ball with a dead bat. His temperament was just right for an opener, and he developed an array of attacking strokes that he used unmercifully after first drawing a bowler's sting with resolute and disciplined batting. Recovering from a war-time broken arm that threatened his career and forced a change of style, Hutton became the first professional this century to captain England, and under his leadership from 1952 to 1955 England never lost a Test series.

Hutton had been a household name in any country where cricket is played since the 1938 Test against Australia at The Oval when he was at the wicket for 800 minutes compiling a then world-record 364 runs. That marathon innings captured the single-minded determination and tenacity that he took into his role as captain. There have been more charasmatic captains, and skippers with a more imaginative and enterprising approach to the game. But few have been able to match Hutton for purposeful leadership and unyielding concentration.

He started his Test career with a duck and 1 against New Zealand at Lord's in 1937, but the selectors remained faithful and he rewarded them in the next Test with a century. From then on he emerged as England's premier batsman and he continually knocked the shine off the new ball to lay the foundation on which many great England totals were built. It was the Australians who always brought out the best in him, perhaps because they had a similar competitive approach to the game he served so well.

There were few more enthralling sights in cricket than Hutton facing Lindwall or Miller on the first morning of a Test match when they were firing on all cylinders and Hutton was in his most determined mood. He averaged a remarkable 88.83 runs on the England tour of Australia in 1950-51, which was more than 50 ahead of any of his team-mates. Again in 1953 he topped the England batting averages with 55.37, this despite the responsibility of being captain. Not only did he lead the England team that regained the Ashes but he was captain of the tour team that retained them in Australia in 1954-55. His long-running opening partnership with Cyril Washbrook was a reliable feature of England cricket teams in 27 Test matches. Hutton's reward of a knighthood could not have gone to a more deserving character who always led his country with pride, dignity and, above all, determination. *Test record:* 79 Tests, 6,971 runs (average: 55.54), 19 centuries, 57 catches. Captain in 23 Tests (won 11, lost 4, drew 8).

TOM GRAVENEY: 'I have to be honest and say that as much as I admired Len Hutton as a player and as a captain I found it hard to get on his wave-length as a person. We were just not each other's cup of tea. My approach to cricket was far too carefree for his taste. I have always held the opinion that cricket is a game to be enjoyed regardless of the pressures. Len tended to treat cricket as if it were life or death. While I recognized the debt England owed him for his strong, firm leadership I thought he was too eaten up by the game and he used to allow himself to be pushed into morose moods by team problems that he insisted on carrying on his own shoulders without trying to share them with his senior players. Len was a difficult man to understand because you never knew quite where you stood with him. One moment he would be a charming companion who could cause a chuckle with his whimsical humour, the next he would look straight through you as if you were a pane of glass. I don't think he was deliberately rude. It was just that he would withdraw into himself and brood about the next session of play. He could become blinkered and obstinate and unwilling, or unable, to see another point of view.

By the time I played with him he had been forced to change his batting style because of a shortened arm caused by a wartime injury. Even with this handicap he was a true master of the batting arts, uneasy only against short-pitched fast bowling when his naturally cautious manner would trigger a defensive shot that invariably led to him offering catches to short leg fielders. I rated myself as pretty fair at the cover drive but I would bow the knee to Hutton as the king of this classic stroke. Never have I seen the shot played the way Len used to play it. He would sweep the bat majestically away from his body in a full arc and the ball would rocket away towards the boundary. That was a really exhilarating sight. But generally Len used to be anchored by caution and it is my personal view that he would have been an even more effective batsman and skipper had he loosened up a little and been more relaxed both on and off the field. He was unquestionably one of the most gifted cricketers ever to lift a cricket bat, yet I felt that there were times when he did not do himself full justice. He could dominate almost any attack yet often allowed himself to be pushed into a defensive shell by bowlers of just moderate ability.

It may seem odd – unkind, even – to be so frank about Hutton more than 30 years after his brilliant performances for England both as a batsman and as a captain. But if this book is to carry any weight then I must be honest with my assessments. There were not many greater batsmen. There were not many more commanding captains. But I am sure that if he were to have his career over again he would try to *enjoy* the game more.

THE PLAYERS

BILL EDRICH
Born: March 26, 1916. *Died* : April 24, 1986.
Test record: 39 Tests, 2,440 runs (average: 40)
6 centuries, 41 wickets (average: 41.29), 39 catches.
England have rarely been served by a more determined and brave character than Bill Edrich. As well as for his consistent run-making, he will always be remembered for his fearless hooking against the fastest bowlers. He was a fine all-round batsman who often dug England out of holes with his do-or-die attitude. Edrich was also a lively fast bowler whose pace and penetration was a useful addition to the England attack. He had his greatest season in harness with his Middlesex 'twin' Denis Compton in 1947. Edrich scored 3,539 runs at an average 80.43 with 12 centuries and he also took 67 wickets. A good-class right winger, he played professional football for Norwich and Spurs. Three of his brothers also played County cricket and John Edrich was a cousin. Bill was a battler on and off the pitch and he was awarded the DFC for wartime bombing raids over Germany.

TOM GRAVENEY
Born: June 16, 1927.
Test record: 79 Tests, 4,882 runs (average: 44.38)
11 centuries, 80 catches.
We have left it to Willie Rushton – self-confessed cricket addict – to provide the analysis of our expert summarizer Tom Graveney. This is how Lord's Taverner Willie introduced him when Tom appeared as his witness on the ITV series *Who's the Greatest?*: 'This is the man who scored 122 centuries including 11 in 79 Tests…He topped 1,000 runs in a season 21 times and was the first batsman to score a a century of centuries in post-war cricket. Now a highly-respected cricket commentator, he was a master off his front foot – indeed, all round the wicket. In fact he was such an elegant player that I fully expected him to arrive at the wicket wearing top hat and tails.' (Tom was a thoughtful tactician who captained Gloucestershire, Worcestershire and, briefly, England. He was a great favourite in Australia where he lived for a spell while serving Queensland as player-coach. His highest Test score was 258 for England against the West Indies at Trent Bridge in 1957. He shared a record fourth wicket stand of 402 with Willie Watson when playing for the MCC against British Guyana in 1953-54. His contribution was 231. Tom scored two centuries in a match on four occasions.)

42

DENIS COMPTON
Born: May 23, 1918.
Test record: 78 Tests, 5,807 runs (average: 50.06)
17 centuries, 25 wickets (average: 56.40), 49 catches.

Denis was the natural, free-flowing genius of English cricket. He was handicapped by recurring knee problems and past his 'Golden Boy' peak by the time of the 1953 series, yet he was still a worry to the Australians who always breathed a sigh of relief when he was on his way back to the pavilion. He electrified matches by his presence at the wicket and he had the ablity to turn a game on its head with an innings of swashbuckling yet graceful wizardry. Compton made more than 1,000 runs in a season 17 times, but it was one particular year – 1947 – when he cemented his place in the record books. In that magical summer of '47 he scored 3,816 runs at an average of 90.85, including a record 18 centuries and 753 runs against South Africa in a five-match series. He was also an inconsistent but occasionally inspired left-arm slow bowler who could conjure a 'chinaman' as a bewildering speciality. Denis was the sportsman that every hero-worshipping schoolboy wanted to emulate. As well as being a brilliant cricketer he was an outstanding footballer who won a 1950 FA Cup winners' medal as a left winger for Arsenal and 14 wartime caps for England. His brother, Leslie, was an accomplished wicket keeper with Middlesex and a powerful Arsenal and England centre-half.

TREVOR BAILEY
Born : December 3, 1923.
Test record: 61 Tests, 2,290 runs (average: 29.74)
1 century, 132 wickets (average: 29.21), 32 catches.

Trevor Bailey emerged as a rival to Alec Bedser as the unofficial 'Man of the Series' with a succession of great and gritty performances. His indomitable spirit shone through in every match and acted as an inspiration to the entire England team. While it was Bailey's often boring but always meaningful batting that took the eye, he was also a first-rate fast-medium bowler who could outwit the greatest batsmen with his late out-swinger. In helpful conditions he could be devastating as he proved against the West Indies in 1954 when he returned his best Test bowling figures of 7 for 34. He was also an outstanding fielder but he will be best remembered for his stubborn, determined batting that earned him the nickname 'Barnacle Bailey'. A double Blue at Cambridge at cricket and football, Trevor captained his beloved Essex from 1961 until 1967. He is now a respected journalist and popular member of the BBC radio commentary team.

WILLIE WATSON
Born: March 7, 1920.
Test record: 23 Tests, 879 runs (average: 25.85)
2 centuries, 8 catches.

He was a graceful left-handed batsman who never quite fulfilled his potential in the Test match arena. Watson liked to attack the bowling from the start of his innings and possessed a wide range of elegant strokes. He made 1,000 runs in a season 14 times while serving Yorkshire and Leicestershire with distinction. Willie was also an outstanding footballer and won four England caps while playing for Huddersfield Town and then Sunderland. His greatest performance came in his debut against Australia when his 109 in a memorable marathon stand with Trevor Bailey saved the game for England. He emigrated to Johannesburg in 1968 to take up a new career as a coach.

REG SIMPSON
Born: February 27, 1920.
Test record: 27 Tests, 1,401 runs (average: 33.35)
4 centuries, 2 wickets (average: 11), 5 catches.

Reg Simpson was a talented right-handed opening batsman and a superb athletic fielder. There have been few batsman to match him for mastering hostile new ball bowling. Born in Robin Hood territory of Sherwood, he became a great favourite at Nottinghamshire where he was captain for nine years. His finest display for England came in the final Melbourne Test of the 1950-51 tour when his undefeated 156 laid the foundation for England's first victory over Australia for 13 years.

JOHNNY WARDLE
Born: January 8, 1923. *Died:* July 23, 1985.
Test record: 653 runs (average: 19.78)
102 wickets (average: 20.39), 12 catches.

Johnny Wardle was one of the great post-war orthodox left-arm spinners who developed the 'chinaman' to such a degree of accuracy that he could be almost unplayable on a turning wicket. He did, however, bowl quite a high percentage of loose balls when he was varying his wrist-spin deliveries, and his figures sometimes suffered. A hard-hitting late-order batsman and a fearless close fielder, he took 100 wickets in a season ten times. Wardle played his cricket with cheerful determination and he often had spectators and players roaring with laughter at his clowning antics. His first-class career ended in controversy when he was sacked by Yorkshire after publicly criticizing their leadership in a newspaper article.

GODFREY EVANS
Born: August 18, 1920.
Test record: 91 Tests, 2,439 runs (average: 20.49)
2 centuries, 173 catches, 46 stumpings.
For sheer exuberance, enthusiasm and match-winning brilliance, 'Godders' was a one-off. He was, without a doubt, the most exciting wicket keeper of all time. Whether he was plucking a spectacular catch out of the air, or whipping off the bails in a lightning quick movement, Godfrey was a joy to watch. He was fearless behind the stumps and would stand up to men as quick as Alec Bedser without losing any of his skill or composure. Evans was also an accomplished batsman, who could be a sheet anchor or aggressive as the situation demanded. He once failed by just two runs to score a century before lunch in the Lord's Test against India, but showed the stubborn side of his nature when going a world record 95 minutes without scoring while his partner Denis Compton plundered the runs to rescue England from a crisis in the 1946-47 Adelaide Test.

JIM LAKER
(see Peter May's England, 1956.)

ALEC BEDSER
Born: July 4, 1918.
Test record: 51 Tests, 714 runs (average: 12.75)
236 wickets (average: 24.89), 26 catches.
English cricket has never had a better servant than Alec Bedser. He was England's most prolific wicket taker for nine years from 1946, and he won several Tests practically on his own. He took five wickets in a Test innings on 15 occasions and claimed ten wickets in a Test five times. His best series was the 1953 rubber against Australia when he took 39 wickets in the five Tests and his bowling was the key factor in England winning the Ashes. Alec, along with his twin brother Eric, was also an effective and influential member of the Surrey team that won seven successive County championships. His main bowling weapon was an in-swinger that continually had batsmen in difficulties but his deadliest delivery was a leg-cutter that moved like a fast leg-break. Added to the penetration of these wicked deliveries, Alec had exceptional line and length, great control and the biggest heart in cricket. As a tail-end batsman he could produce stubborn resistance, particularly when charged with the nightwatchman's responsibilities. Since his retirement in 1960 Alec has continued to serve English cricket as a selector and he had a long run as chairman of the selectors.

THEY ALSO SERVED

DON KENYON
Born: May 15, 1924.
Test record: 8 Tests, 192 runs (average: 12.80), 5 catches.
He was an accomplished right-handed opening batsman and a prolific run-maker for Worcestershire but, like so many openers, had to live in the shadow of the great Len Hutton. His greatest moments came with Worcestershire. He was County captain for nine years and led them to two successive championship successes in the mid-60s.

PETER MAY
(see Peter May's England, 1956.)

TONY LOCK
(see Peter May's England, 1956.)

FREDDIE BROWN
Born: December 16, 1910.
Test record: 22 Tests, 734 runs (average: 25.31)
45 wickets (average: 31.06), 22 catches.
He was a powerfully built, big-hearted all-rounder who played the game with great enthusiasm and energy. A hammering right-handed batsman and a useful medium-pace bowler, he had spells as captain of England and Northamptonshire and was chairman of the selectors when he made a one-Test comeback during the 1953 series at the age of forty-two.

FRED TRUEMAN
(see Peter May's England, 1956.)

BRIAN STATHAM
(see Peter May's England, 1956.)

ROY TATTERSALL
Born: August 17, 1922.
Test record: 16 Tests, 50 runs (average: 5)
58 wickets (average: 26.08), 8 catches.
Roy Tattersall was a right-arm off-spin bowler of the highest quality, but was kept out of the Test side for much of his career by Jim Laker. He was not a great spinner of the ball, but used flight and variation of pace to deceive the batsmen. He was a loyal and dedicated Lancashire player and took more than 100 wickets in a season eight times.

THE TOM GRAVENEY ASSESSMENT

You need first to appreciate the depths to which English cricket confidence had sunk to understand the euphoria that surrounded our victory over Australia in the magnificent 1953 series. England had been buried out of sight by Don Bradman's 1948 wonders and it was 19 years since we had won the Ashes, the historic prize against which all our achievements were measured. We were desperate for an Ashes victory to rid ourselves of an 'Aussie complex' that had been brought on by the magnificent tandem team of Lindwall and Miller and a procession of brilliant batsmen.

I have to confess that my form with the bat in that summer of '53 did not really warrant me playing throughout the series. I had been so determined not to fall victim to the pace of Lindwall and Miller that I experimented with a new style that reduced my ability to score on the off-side, but at least my technique of getting right behind the ball proved effective against pace and so I kept my place in a team buoyed by the brilliance of Bedser and the bravery of Bailey. Len Hutton's consistent batting and his firm, authoritative leadership were key factors in a series in which the Aussies deserve much praise for their totally committed and sporting attitude. Every Test was fought tooth and nail but good sportsmanship never once took a back seat. The weather was the only let-down throughout a series that was a thriller from first ball to last, and I often wonder what the outcome might have been had the Australians had a spinner in the Laker-Lock class to take advantage of what were often wet and dodgy wickets. If I can be critical at this distance, I remain puzzled as to why the selectors played the immensely promising Peter May in only three Tests and did not call up the young, fiery Fred Trueman until the fifth and deciding Test when his pace at last brought penetration to our attack and gave Bedser the support he so desperately needed.

Even more than 30 years on my spine tingles at the memory of that marvellous final Test when we clinched the Ashes victory. The emotion-charged atmosphere at the ground was simply unbelievable and the country just about came to a halt as people gathered around their television and wireless sets to watch and listen to the final day's play. The Australians were marvellous in defeat and I recall foggily how both teams celebrated at a party afterwards during which Lindsay Hassett showed the unerring accuracy of all Australian fieldsmen by hitting the clock on the wall with a half-pint mug. The match finished at three o'clock in the afternoon. I arrived home at three o'clock the next morning. Ah, happy days!

Peter May's England, 1956

THE SQUAD:

Peter Richardson (5)	Cyril Washbrook (3)	Alan Oakman (2)
Colin Cowdrey (5)	Trevor Bailey (4)	Tony Lock (4)
David Sheppard (2)	Willie Watson (1)	Fred Trueman (2)
Peter May (5)	Godfrey Evans (5)	Bob Appleyard (1)
Denis Compton (1)	Jim Laker (5)	Brian Statham (1)
Tom Graveney (2)	Johnny Wardle (1)	Alan Moss (1)
Doug Insole (1)	Frank Tyson (1)	

SCOREBOARD: 5 Tests, 2 wins, 1 defeat, 2 draws

Figures in brackets indicate the number of Test match appearances

---

BACKGROUND

We need to go to a County match at The Oval in May 1956 for curtain-raising facts on one of the most sensational and controversial series in Test cricket history. Surrey were playing the Australian tourists in an early-season match and won by 10 wickets to become the first County side for 44 years to triumph over an Australian team. That in itself was quite remarkable, but what made the victory even more extraordinary was the manner in which it was obtained. Jim Laker was the author of Australia's downfall, taking all 10 wickets in the first innings for 88 runs with skilful off-spin bowling that had the Aussie batsmen looking, as the hit song of the time said, "bewitched, bothered and bewildered".*

In the second innings, the Australians collapsed to the left-arm spin conjured by Tony Lock who took 7 for 49—quite a contrast to his 0 for 100 in the first innings. Australian skipper

---

*It was the first time that a bowler had taken all 10 Australian wickets since Surrey left-arm spinner Edward Barratt had finished with 10 for 43 while representing the Players against the tourists at The Oval in 1878.

Ian Johnson, the No. 1 off-spinner for the tourists, bowled a marathon 60-over spell in Surrey's first innings and finished with figures of 6 for 168. He flighted the ball beautifully, but on pitching he got little response with his off-breaks. It was obvious that he was not in the Laker-Lock league for getting the most out of a turning English wicket.

Surrey's success alerted the England selectors to the fact that spin could be a winning hand in the coming Test series and in Laker and Lock they had two aces.

TOM GRAVENEY: 'On an English wicket, I would have backed Laker and Lock against any spin combination. Laker relied on uncannily accurate length and flight as reinforcements to his fizzing spin, while Lock pushed the ball through so quickly that if he got movement off the pitch you just could not play the ball with any confidence at all. In fact Tony was sometimes as fast as a "quickie" and he was often on the receiving end of accusations that he threw rather than bowled his faster ball. It was strange how a transformation had come into the game, because the theory had always been that off-spin bowling was like food and drink to the Australian batsmen. That was why the likes of a magnificent craftsman like Tom Goddard got so few Test opportunities in pre-war Tests against the Aussies who used to take England off-spinners apart. But by the time the 1956 series came around the Australian batsman had got out of the habit of facing off-spin, and just the appearance of Laker and Lock on the same field seemed to induce sheer panic. On the 1954-55 tour to Australia we had undermined the Aussies with the sheer blinding pace of Frank Tyson. He was injured for much of the summer of '56, but Laker and Lock were ready with a slow torture that caused the Australians just about the worst humiliation of their lives.'

THE OPPOSITION

Ian Johnson led an Australian side that had several players – Lindwall, Miller and wicket keeper Gil Langley, for instance – deep into the sunset of their golden careers. They were desperately unlucky throughout the tour with a succession of injury problems that prevented them from finding a a settled side, but in the final analysis their defeat in the series came about because they were just not good enough to master an England team that had better all-round strength. Their batting in particular

49

left a lot to be desired. Opener Jim Burke topped their averages at the end of the five Tests with 30.11, with Richie Benaud second on 25.00. Their players did not have one Test century to show between them at the end of the low-scoring series. A lot of responsibility rested on the shoulders of the usually majestic Neil Harvey, but the left-hander rarely got his timing right in the Tests and he finished with a disappointing average of 19.70.

THE TEST MATCHES
FIRST TEST: Trent Bridge (June 7-12)

Rain washed out more than 12 hours of play and even two declarations by Peter May could not force a positive result. There was just a hint of what was to come later in the summer when Laker and Lock claimed between them 10 of the 12 Australian wickets that fell during the match. A feature of the game was two solid opening partnerships of 53 and 171 by Peter Richardson and Colin Cowdrey. Richardson became the first batsman to score 50 in each innings of his Test debut against Australia without reaching a 100 in either of them. He was out for 81 and then 73. Australia, handicapped by injuries to both Lindwall and Davidson, were set a target of 258 to win in the final four hours. They made no attempt to chase the runs and a stop-start match petered out into a tame draw. **RESULT: Match drawn. England 217 for 8 dec. and 188 for 3 dec., Australia 148 and 120 for 3.**

SECOND TEST: Lord's (June 21-26)

Keith Miller and wicket keeper Gil Langley emerged as the match heroes as Australia produced their best performance of the tour to win comfortably by 185 runs. Ian Johnson won the toss for the only time in the series and Colin McDonald (78) and Jim Burke (65) celebrated his decision to bat with a superb first wicket stand of 137 that laid the foundation for victory. It was the highest opening stand by Australia against England since 1930. England's problems started when Cowdrey was out to a magnificent catch by Richie Benaud. May (63) and Trevor Bailey (32) apart, the England batsmen failed to put up real resistance against inspired bowling by Miller (5-72) and they were all out for 171. Fred Trueman (5-90) bowled England back into the match, but then a lightning strike from Richie Benaud (97), balanced by a painstaking contribution from the stubborn Ken 'Slasher' Mackay (32), reasserted Australia's hold on the game. England never looked like getting within hitting distance of their victory target of

372 and only Peter May (53) reached a half-century. Miller (5-80) took 10 wickets in a Test for the only time in his career and proved that even at 36 he was still a potent force. He was aided and abetted by Gil Langley who established a world Test record with nine dismissals. **RESULT: Australia (285 and 257) beat England (171 and 186) by 185 runs.**

THIRD TEST: Headingley (July 12-17)

The England selectors recalled 41-year-old Cyril Washbrook after an absence from the Test arena of five years. The doyen of Lancashire cricket – himself a selector – could not have had a more challenging recall. He came to the wicket in England's first innings with the scoreboard at 17 for 3, and proceeded to put on 187 for the fourth wicket in partnership with skipper May (101). Washbrook's contribution was just two short of his century when he was trapped lbw by Benaud. This stand was not only the turning point of the match but also of the rubber as Laker and Lock spun England to their first ever victory over Australia at Headingley. Only Jim Burke (41), Keith Miller (41) and Richie Benaud (30) played with any real confidence as the tourists failed to save the follow-on. In their second innings Neil Harvey (69) produced his only really telling innings of the series, showing his true ability as he sealed up one end despite the umbrella of English close fielders hungering for just one slip. But even Harvey's brilliant innings was not enough to save Australia from an innings defeat. Laker finished with match figures of 11 for 113 off 70.3 overs, an exceptional performance that he was to make look rather average a fortnight later. **RESULT: England (325) beat Australia (143 and 140) by an innings and 42 runs.**

FOURTH TEST: Old Trafford (July 26-31)

This has gone down in history as 'Laker's Match' following a bowling performance that is never likely to be equalled, or even approached. England won the toss and elected to bat first on what looked a brown but sound pitch. They accumulated 459 runs in 491 minutes, with Peter Richardson and the recalled David Sheppard – now the Bishop of Liverpool – each scoring centuries after Colin Cowdrey had opened with 80. Then Laker took the stage with the most successful spell of bowling there has ever been. McDonald and Burke gave Australia a steady start in their first innings and they were 62 for 2 at tea on the second day. At the close of the day's play they were following on at 51 for 1 in their second innings! Laker had destroyed them with seven wickets for eight runs in 22 balls. Heavy rain interruptions raised Australian hopes of saving the match but then Laker became unplayable on the churned-up pitch, particularly when the sun shone through the heavy cloud on the afternoon of the fifth and final day. Only McDonald, with a battling 89, managed to defy Laker as Australia collapsed from 112 for 2 to 205 all out and defeat by an innings and 170 runs. Laker had taken all 10 second innings wickets at a personal cost of 53 runs, and he finished with the astonishing match figures of 19 for 90. Tony Lock bowled one more over than the 68 from Laker but was able to take only one wicket. All of Laker's wickets were taken from the Stretford End on a ground where there had not been a definite Ashes result since 1905. Records galore as well as wickets tumbled to Laker. His 19 wickets were the most taken in a first-class match; it was the first time that 10 wickets had been claimed in a Test match; it was the only instance of 10 wickets in a match twice in the same season; his 39 wickets in a rubber equalled the record set in 1953 by his old Surrey colleague Alec Bedser, and there was still one more Test to be played. The Australians muttered angrily about the pitch being doctored, but there was no doubt that they had been well and truly Lakered. **RESULT: England (459) beat Australia (84 and 205) by an innings and 170 runs.**

FIFTH TEST: The Oval (August 23-28)

Rain interruptions accounted for the loss of more than 12 hours play, just as in the first Test. Laker – with 4 for 80 and 3 for 8 – lifted his series haul to a record 46 wickets. The England selectors again made an inspired recall, bringing Denis Compton – minus a right knee cap – back into the firing line. He was top scorer in England's first innings with 94 before becoming one of medium-pacer Ron Archer's five victims. He put on 156 for the third wicket with the consistent May (86 not out) who finished the series with a splendid average of 90.60. Harvey took over behind the stumps after Gil Langley had been struck on the head by a ball from Archer. Miller (61) was top scorer in Australia's reply of 202 – 45 short of England's total. Heavy rain washed out the fourth day's play and May delayed a declaration until just after four o'clock on the final day. A draw looked a formality but then Australia got themselves into all sorts of difficulties against the spin of Laker and Lock and were in trouble at 27 for 5 at the close, leaving May pondering on what might have been had he made an earlier declaration. **RESULT: Match drawn. England 247 and 182-3 dec., Australia 202 and 27-5.**

THE CAPTAIN

Peter May was out of the classical school of English cricket – Charterhouse and Cambridge University – and is generally acclaimed as England's greatest post-war batsman. Born in Reading, Berkshire, on New Year's Eve 1929, he was an immaculate stroke maker who compiled 4,537 Test runs at an average 46.77. His tapestry of magical performances included 13 Test centuries and a magnificent unbeaten 285 against the West Indies at Edgbaston in 1957. He took over the England captaincy from Len Hutton in 1955 and was skipper for a record reign of 41 Tests, and on his way to 66 Test appearances equalled Frank Woolley's then world record of 52 consecutive Test matches. He was dogged by ill health in the second half of his career and retired at the all too early age of thirty-one, leaving behind him a procession of wrecked bowling averages and a collection of some of the finest innings ever witnessed anywhere in the world. He was a prolific scorer in County cricket for Surrey and took over as skipper from Stuart Surridge for the last two years of Surrey's 1950s' sequence of seven successive Championship victories. He became a successful businessman in the world of insurance, and he has served as a Test selector and also as chairman of the selectors. *Test record:* 66 Tests, 4,537 runs, average 46.77, 13 centuries, 42 catches. Captain in 41 Tests (won 20, lost 10, drew 11).

TOM GRAVENEY: 'Peter May was out of the same mould as his predecessor Len Hutton – a master of the batting arts, and, as a captain, a strict disciplinarian who set and expected exceptionally high standards. As with Hutton, I didn't really hit it off with May because my attitude was a little too casual for his liking, but that did nothing to lessen my admiration of him as a supreme batsman. Peter learned his captaincy under two contrasting characters – Stuart Surridge at Surrey and Hutton in the Test arena. The dynamic, exuberant Surridge appeared to have less influence on his protege than the cautious, competitive Hutton. Peter could be a real tiger in the field, ticking off anybody if he thought they were giving something less than total effort and concentration. Yet for a man who came alive the moment he strode imperiously on to a pitch, he was strangely shy and uncommunicative away from the field of play. This was his weakness as a captain because it meant he was unable to give a team – particularly when on tour – the moulding leadership that it needs. It was a tragedy for English cricket that he chose to retire so early, at a time when most cricketers are in full bloom. As a batsman, he had no equal in the English game. Had he stayed in the game I believe he would have rewritten the record books. He was a dictator of bowlers despite his lack of arrogance and I often wonder just how more effective he might have been had he had a little devilment inside him. He hit the ball with colossal power to all points of the compass, yet always retaining style and grace. There have, in my opinion, been players better equipped to captain Test teams, but every Englishman has to bow the knee to Peter May as a batsman.

THE PLAYERS

PETER RICHARDSON
Born : July 4, 1931.
Test record: 34 Tests, 2,061 runs (average: 37.47)
5 centuries, 3 wickets (average: 16), 6 catches.
Peter Richardson was from a talented cricketing family and the eldest of three brothers, all of whom played County cricket. He was a steady accumulator of runs as a left-handed opening batsman, first with Worcestershire and then Kent. His good humour made him popular in the dressing-room, and his skill at steering the ball through the tightest fields earned him the respect of colleagues and opponents alike. He topped 2,000 runs in a season four times and beat the 1,000-run mark 12 times.

COLIN COWDREY
Born : December 24, 1932.
Test record: 114 Tests, 7,624 runs (average: 44.06)
22 centuries, 120 catches.
If anybody was born to be a cricketer it was Colin Cowdrey. His father deliberately saw to it that he had the initials M.C.C., and he was gathering runs almost as soon as he could walk. A masterly batsman with excellent technique, he played in a world record 114 Tests and scored more than 1,000 runs 27 times on his way to a career total of 42,719. He was a prolific run-maker for Oxford University before continuing his distinguished 26-year career with Kent. Colin scored 22 Test centuries and delighted crowds throughout the world with his style and elegance at the wicket. He was always dignified and sporting regardless of the pressure on him and was a marvellous ambassador for England wherever he played. A brilliant slip fielder with sharp reflexes and safe hands, he held 120 catches in Test matches. He succeeded Peter May as England skipper and led them to eight victories in 27 Tests, with 15 draws and four defeats. Tom

Graveney rates him the best captain under whom he ever toured, particularly in the West Indies in 1967-68, a series that England won 1-0 with four Tests drawn. His one disappointment was that he was never appointed captain for a tour of Australia where he was one of the most popular of all English players. He captained Kent from 1957 until 1971 and lifted the County championship in 1970. Two of his sons, Christopher and Graham, are carving out promising careers with Kent. He remains a respected figure in the cricket world and has been President of the MCC.

DAVID SHEPPARD
Born: March 6, 1929.
Test record: 22 Tests, 1,172 runs (average: 37.80)
 3 centuries, 12 catches.
Now the Bishop of Liverpool, David was the first ordained minister to play in Test cricket. He was a graceful off-side player and an opener of the highest calibre who had enormous powers of concentration. A thoughtful captain of Cambridge University and Sussex, he amassed 45 centuries during a career to which he was never able to give his total attention because of his religious calling. His 1,000 runs for Cambridge in 1950 included two marathon opening stands with John Dewes – 343 against the West Indies and 349 against Sussex. He underlined his immense potential in 1952 when he finished top of the national batting averages with 2,262 runs at an average 64.62. In the same season he made his Test debut against India, and scored his first century for England at The Oval. While reading for holy orders, he twice captained England against Pakistan in 1954 when Len Hutton was indisposed. A brilliant 113 in the second innings of the Melbourne Test in 1962-63 lifted England to their only victory of the series. Tom Graveney recalls how David dropped a couple of catches off the bowling of Fred Trueman in Australia. Trueman said with his cutting Yorkshire humour that had even Sheppard roaring with laughter: 'It's a pity, Reverend, that you don't put your hands together more often in t'field.'

CYRIL WASHBROOK
Born: December 6, 1914.
Test record: 37 Tests, 2,569 runs (average: 42.81)
6 centuries, 12 catches.
Cyril Washbrook was a consistent and attractive right-handed opening batsman, who had a very sound defensive technique but was an attacking batsman by nature. He was especially severe on anything short of a length and was a fearless hooker and puller. He is best remembered for his formidable opening partnership

with Len Hutton that stretched across 27 Test matches. They were the finest foundation builders for England since the golden days of Hobbs and Sutcliffe. Cyril, one of the best cover-point fielders in post-war cricket, was a loyal servant to Lancashire throughout his career during which he scored over 34,000 first-class runs. He was the first professional to skipper Lancashire, and he became an England selector and made a successful comeback to Test cricket at the age of forty-one during the memorable 1956 series against Australia.

TREVOR BAILEY
(see Len Hutton's England, 1953.)

GODFREY EVANS
(see Len Hutton's England, 1953.)

TONY LOCK
Born: July 5, 1929.
Test record: 49 Tests, 742 runs (average: 13.74)
 174 wickets (average: 25.58), 59 catches.
Tony Lock was one of the most competitive and inspiring spin bowlers of all time. He had a fiery spirit to go with his thinning red hair and he used to spill over with the sort of aggression and totally committed attitude more associated with pace bowlers. All batsmen were his natural enemy. He was an orthodox slow left-arm bowler who used to vary his pace from slow to almost fast-medium. His quicker ball used to cause controversy because of a suspicion of a throw, but he was just as effective with his slow deliveries that could produce sharp turn and lift, accompanied by some expressive gestures and colourful language. Along with his spin twin, Jim Laker, he played a prominent part in making Surrey the dominant county of the 1950s. He was also a useful lower-order batsman and an outstanding short leg fielder who took 59 catches in Tests and once pouched eight catches in a county match against Warwickshire in 1957. His highest score with the bat (89) came in his final England appearance when he and Pat Pocock shared a record 109 ninth wicket partnership against the West Indies in Georgetown in 1967-68. In a remarkable extension to his career he emigrated to Australia and skippered Western Australia to the Sheffield Shield and set a new wicket-taking record for the State. He returned to England in the mid-1960s for a lively spell as captain of Leicestershire. He had an army of fans in Perth who used to chant during any quiet moment in a match: 'Put Lockie on.' Wherever he played he brought electricity and entertainment to the cricket stage.

JIM LAKER

Born: February 9, 1922. *Died:* April 23 1986.
Test record: 46 Tests, 676 runs (average: 14.08)
193 wickets (average: 21.24), 12 catches.

Jim Laker's 19 wickets for 90 in the 1956 Old Trafford Test will stand for all time as a statistical monument to his genius. He had a model action and he rarely strayed from a perfect line and length. He always gave the ball a real tweak and non-striking batsmen could almost hear it hum like a spinning top as it left his fingers. His most productive season was 1950 when his haul of 166 wickets included incredible figures of 8 for 2 in the Test trial at Bradford. He spun the ball sharply in any conditions and there has rarely, if ever, been a bowler better equipped to exploit helpful wickets. Jim was also a very useful late-order batsman and a dependable gully fielder. Yorkshire-born, he had an outstanding career with Surrey for whom he was a key man in their team that won seven successive county championships. He could be waspish with his opinions and fell out with the Establishment at the back end of his career. He played briefly for Essex before becoming a greatly respected television commentator and journalist.

FRED TRUEMAN

Born: February 6, 1931.
Test record: 67 Tests, 981 runs (average: 13.81)
307 wickets (average: 21.57), 64 catches.

Fred Trueman was (and is) one of the great characters of English cricket. His nickname –'Fiery Fred'– summed him up as a competitor and cricketer. He was a fast, hostile and tenacious bowler whose colourful character and strong will to win made him a national hero when he at last brought pace and penetration to the England attack after the selectors had for years put too much responsibility on the broad shoulders of Alec Bedser. Early in his career, he was often wild with his deliveries when he relied mainly on sheer pace and hostility generated by his long curved run and classic action. But he gradually brought accuracy and clever change of pace and direction to his bowling. The Trueman yorker was a deadly and spectacular sight to see, and in later years he perfected the art of swing bowling and used his bouncer more sparingly as a lethal weapon. He was a controversial character whose on-field ferociousness and strong language often got him into trouble with selectors and captains who struggled to tether his explosive temperament. A competent right-handed late-order batsman, he could strike the ball with real power, and his fielding at short leg was always efficient and at times electrifying. When patrolling in the deep his throwing arm was so strong that few batsmen chanced taking a run once he had reached the ball. Mellowed in middle age, he is now an outspoken commentator and cricket columnist.

BRIAN STATHAM
Born: June 16, 1930.
Test record: 70 Tests, 675 runs (average: 11.44)
252 wickets (average: 24.82), 28 catches.
Brian – or George, as he was known to his team-mates – was a consistent performer at the highest level for more than 15 years and was the unsung hero of English cricket in the 1950s and early 1960s. He was a classical fast bowler whose nagging accuracy set batsmen up for the 'kill' by partners like Fred Trueman and Frank Tyson. They were more hostile but could not match Brian's deadly length and line. He was a captain's dream, always prepared to bowl himself into the ground for his team. He was also a brilliant deep field and an occasionally adventurous left-handed tail-end batsman.

THEY ALSO SERVED

DENIS COMPTON
(see Len Hutton's England, 1953.)

ALAN OAKMAN
Born: April 20, 1930.
Test record: 2 Tests, 14 runs (average: 7), 7 catches.
Alan Oakman was a competent right handed batsman, a reliable off-break bowler and a close fielder of the highest standard. He played in two Tests in 1956 and was outstanding in the field where he took seven catches, all off the bowling of Jim Laker.

TOM GRAVENEY
(see Len Hutton's England, 1953).

DOUG INSOLE
Born: April 18, 1926.
Test record: 9 Tests, 408 runs (average: 27.20)
1 century, 8 catches.
Doug was an aggressive and competitive right-handed batsman, a medium-pace bowler and an excellent field and on top of his gifts as an all-rounder he had one of the finest tactical brains in cricket. He captained Cambridge University in 1949, and led Essex from

1950 to 1960. He topped 1,000 runs in a season 13 times. Doug was a fine footballer who captained Cambridge and won an FA Amateur Cup medal at Wembley with Corinthian Casuals. An able administrator, he has been chairman of the T.C.C.B.

FRANK TYSON
Born: June 6, 1930.
Test record: 17 Tests, 230 runs (average: 10.95)
76 wickets (average: 18.56), 4 catches.
Frank Tyson, at his peak, was possibly the fastest bowler of all-time. In 1954-55, England convincingly beat Australia by three Tests to one, mainly thanks to devastating bowling that earned Tyson the nickname 'Typhoon'. Roaring in off a long run, he generated tremendous pace that unnerved and unhinged even the greatest batsmen. He was plagued by injury throughout his all too brief career and was forced into retirement in 1960 after just eight years of first-class cricket.

WILLIE WATSON
(see Len Hutton's England, 1953.)

BOB APPLEYARD
Born: June 27, 1924.
Test record: 9 Tests, 51 runs (average: 17)
31 wickets (average: 25.41), 4 catches.
A much under-rated player, Bob Appleyard was a medium-paced off-spinner whose mixture of spin and speed made him a difficult bowler to master, particularly on any wicket that offered him encouragement. But for ill-health and the presence of bowlers like Laker, Lock and Wardle, he would have been better established as a star-quality bowler.

JOHNNY WARDLE
(see Len Hutton's England, 1953.)

ALAN MOSS
Born: November 14, 1930.
Test record: 9 Tests, 61 runs (average: 10.16)
21 wickets (average: 29.80), 1 catch.
Alan Moss was a steady, consistent right-arm fast bowler and featured as the main strike force for Middlesex for over a decade. He played in the first Test of 1956 because of injuries to Trueman, Staham and Tyson. He took 1,301 wickets during a career in which he became respected as much for his accuracy as his speed.

THE TOM GRAVENEY ASSESSMENT

Australia went home at the end of their 1956 tour with Jim Laker stamped all the way through them. He left deep psychological wounds on some of them that never ever healed. There was also a lot of bitterness buried inside them that came to the surface when I made my home in Queensland some years later. One very amiable ex-Australian captain stopped dead a conversation we were having about cricket when the 1956 series was mentioned. 'That series was an affront to sportsmanship,' he said, unable to disguise the anger he felt even at that distance. 'The results should be eliminated from the record books.' The common Australian charge is that England had ordered all the grass to be shaven off the Old Trafford pitch to aid the spin of Laker and Lock in the fourth Test. I don't pretend to know whether this is fact or a figment of bruised Australian imaginations. But I must be candid and admit my suspicions that there just might be something in the allegations.

I was at Manchester the day before the fourth Test started after being selected for the match that I missed because of a hand injury. The pitch then looked good and a trifle greenish. When I returned to Old Trafford on the morning of the match it was nothing but a brown strip, looking tailormade for the sort of deadly spin that Laker and Lock could produce. I remember sitting there watching the morning's play from the pavilion when that great character Keith Miller came bustling up the steps at lunchtime on the first day, saying: 'I'm going to wear my dark glasses after lunch. I've got to keep the sand out of my eyes somehow.' But to counter that there is the story my dear old departed pal Jim Laker told me when all the controversy about the pitch was at its peak. He said that while the two captains were out in the middle tossing the coin he bumped into Sir Donald Bradman, who was travelling with Australia as a team official. The Don said to Jim: 'This is just the sort of wicket we have been waiting for.'

England won the toss and went on to amass a match-winning 459 runs. With that sort of total in the bank, the situation was just made for a great spin artist like Laker. The mystery is how that fine exponent of left-arm spin, Tony Lock, managed to get only one wicket while bowling one more over than Laker. The general theory is that Tony was trying *too* hard, pushing the ball through at a rate of knots and not giving the pitch a chance to play its part. Laker bowled to an exact length and knew exactly where to land and at what pace to get the most vicious turn possible. I always told Jim that he only got his record because injury prevented me from playing. The extremely tall Alan Oakman, a magnificent close field, took my place and held on to five catches in Laker's leg trap.

Regardless of what the Australians say or think about the Old Trafford experience, they have to concede that following the second Test they were outbatted, outfielded and—without question—outbowled. And they had nobody in the class of Jim Laker, whose performances lifted him into the land of cricketing legend.

Richie Benaud's Australia, 1960-61

THE SQUAD:

Colin McDonald (5)	Ken Mackay (5)	Lindsay Kline (2)
Bobby Simpson (5)	Alan Davidson (4)	Johnny Martin (3)
Neil Harvey (4)	Richie Benaud (5)	Frank Misson (3)
Norm O'Neill (5)	Wally Grout (5)	Peter Burge (1)
Les Favell (4)	Ian Meckiff (2)	Des Hoare (1)

SCOREBOARD: 5 Tests, 2 wins, 1 draw, 1 defeat, 1 tie

Figures in brackets indicate the number of Test match appearances

---

BACKGROUND

There was no indication in the early stages of the 1960-61 West Indies tour of Australia that they were on the brink of taking part in, if not the greatest Test series of all time, then certainly the most enthralling and exciting. Richie Benaud's Australians were at their peak after seeing off England, Pakistan and India, while West Indies were rebuilding under the inspired guidance of Frank Worrell following two set-backs against England and a 2-1 series defeat by Pakistan.

West Indies began the tour with a 94-run defeat by Western Australia, but a chanceless 252 by Rohan Kanhai lifted the tourists to a morale-boosting victory over Victoria in their second match during which Sonny Ramadhin suggested that he had recaptured his magical spinning powers. Then the West Indies slumped to an innings defeat by New South Wales, their star player Gary Sobers falling to the bowling of Benaud for a duck. The critics were already writing the West Indies off, and with the first Test in Brisbane just a few days away there seemed little chance that they could find the necessary consistency and cohesion to trouble the powerful Australians.

TOM GRAVENEY: 'That first Test—indeed the entire series—has gone down in cricketing folklore. It was played with a spirit of adventure and sportsmanship that captured not only the interest of record crowds in Australia but the imagination of cricket fans around the world. The series started with the first tie in the history of Test cricket and was not decided until Australia's ninth wicket pair scampered for a bye on the fifth day of the final Test. Both Australia and West Indies showed the way the game could and should be played and the response of the Australian public was quite astonishing. There were massive attendances throughout the series, including a world record 90,800 crowd drawn to Melbourne on the second day of the final Test. A sign of how popular the West Indies became during that tour is that the streets of Melbourne were jammed solid with well wishers when the tourists made a farewell parade through the city in open-topped limousines. We are featuring Richie Benaud's Aussies in this chapter, but Frank Worrell's West Indians deserve equal projection and praise for their contribution to a Test series that will be remembered for as long as cricket is played. It was Frank Worrell who threw down the gauntlet, challenging the Australians to play a thrilling type of cricket in which there was no room for defensive strategy. It was Richie Benaud who had the courage to pick it up and to encourage his players to meet the West Indies head-on in a series that was jam-packed with classic cricket.'

THE OPPOSITION

Frank Worrell was given the job of masterminding a West Indies revival following what, by their skyscraping standards, amounted to a a slump. The other two members of the famous 'three Ws' trio—Everton Weekes and Clyde Walcott—had retired from the Test stage, but Worrell had the luxury of being able to call on the one and only Gary Sobers at his peak, and he had craftsmen of the calibre of Conrad Hunte and Rohan Kanhai to give beef to the batting line-up. He could with great confidence toss the new ball to the fearsome fast bowler Wes Hall, but with Charlie Griffith left behind in the West Indies he often had to take the responsibility himself of sharing the opening attack with his accurate but rarely hostile medium pacers. Ramadhin and Valentine were coming to the end of the Test line as match-winning spinners, but talented off-spinner Lance Gibbs had emerged as a bowler of great craft and cunning who was on his way to what was then a world record haul of 309 Test wickets. On paper, West Indies looked a match for the Australians. And so it proved on the pitch…

THE TEST MATCHES
FIRST TEST: Brisbane (December 10-14, 1960)

Right from the first day, when Sobers scored 132 runs in 174 minutes in a masterpiece of an innings, this was a classic of a contest. Quite fittingly, it was the 500th Test match to be staged. West Indies were all out for 453, Alan Davidson taking 5 for 135 in 30 eight-ball overs. Australia replied with 505, Norm O'Neil top scoring with 181. The Aussies then dismissed West Indies for 284, Davidson again doing the damage with his lethal left-arm pace bowling. He finished with match figures of 11 for 222 and became the first player in Test history to take 10 wickets and score 100 runs in a match. Sobers, 14 in the second innings, collected his 3,000th run in Test cricket. But these impressive statistics were buried in the excitement generated by the events of the final day. Australia were left with 233 runs to win in 310 minutes. They made a disastrous start to their second innings and looked doomed to defeat at 92 for six. Then their two great all-rounders Benaud and Davidson added 134 for the seventh wicket at a run a minute. There were seven minutes left and just seven runs needed for victory when Davidson (80) was run out by Joe Solomon when chasing a quick single.

Wes Hall began the last eight-ball over with Australia needing six to win with three wickets remaining. Wicket keeper Wally Grout scrambled a leg bye off the first ball. Five runs needed. Off the second ball, Benaud attempted a hook shot to the boundary and was caught at the wicket for 52. Six balls left, two wickets to fall and five needed. Ian Meckiff was next in and after making a non-scoring stroke off his first ball ran a bye off the next. Four balls left, four to win. The excited Hall missed a caught-and-bowled chance from Grout off his fifth ball as the batsmen crossed for a single. Meckiff slashed the sixth ball towards the square leg boundary. They ran two but then Grout was run out as he made a despairing dive for a match-winning third run. Two balls left and the scores were level as last man Lindsay Kline faced Hall. He turned his first ball to mid-wicket and as Meckiff came charging in for what he thought would be the winning run sharp-eyed Solomon scored a direct hit on the stumps with an astonishingly accurate throw, considering the immense pressure he was under. This magnificent piece of fielding produced the first tie in the history of Test cricket. Meckiff left the pitch close to tears, convinced Australia had lost. It was some time before Richie Benaud was able to persuade him that he had just played a prominent part in the first-ever tied Test. **RESULT: Match tied. West Indies 453 and 184, Australia 505 and 232.**

Above: Don Bradman comes out to bat at Worcester at the start of the 1948 England tour during which his Australian team was unbeatable.

Right: John Goddard, who experienced both sides of the cricket coin as captain of the West Indies. He led a triumphant team to England in 1950, but was unable to repeat the winning formula seven years later.

Above: Trevor Bailey got his 'Barnacle' nickname because of his stubborn batting, but he was also a naggingly accurate bowler as he proves here by trapping South African Trevor Goddard lbw in a Test match at Port Elizabeth in 1957. Godfrey Evans is the appealing wicket keeper. *Right:* Len Hutton shows his mastery of the late cut during the 1954 Adelaide Test in which England retained the Ashes under his leadership.

Above: Keith Miller, Australia's flamboyant right-handed batsman and a strike bowler who could be deadly when in partnership with Ray Lindwall. It was the Miller-Lindwall tandem team that wrecked England in 1948. *Right:* Ray Lindwall, the Rolls Royce of fast bowlers. He claimed 27 Test wickets on the 1948 tour of England, and his 6-20 return in the final Test was considered one of the finest displays of sustained fast bowling ever seen.

'Those two little friends of mine, Ramadhin and Valentine...' West Indian spin twins Sonny Ramadhin (right) and Alf Valentine (above) inspired the calypso singers as well as their team-mates with bowling that had the England batsmen baffled and bewildered during the 1950 tour.

The 'three Ws' of the West Indies who spelt treble trouble for England's bowlers during the 1950 tour of England: *top left,* Frank Worrell; *top right,* Clyde Walcott; and *right,* Everton Weekes. Worrell was back in England in 1963 as captain of a West Indies team that carried too much pace and power for the side skippered by Ted Dexter. One of the great gentlemen of the game, Worrell was knighted in 1964.

Godfrey Evans, England's wicket keeper in 91 Tests, is warmly remembered as much for his exuberance and enthusiasm as his excellence behind the stumps.

Above: The Middle-sex 'twins' Denis Compton (right) and Bill Edrich prepare to continue their long-running partnership of 1947 during which they compiled 30 centuries between them. *Right:* Compton completes the most memorable shot of his career: the boundary that clinched the regaining of the Ashes at The Oval in 1953.

Peter May, a master batsman out of the classical school, succeeded Len Hutton as England captain and was skipper for a record reign of 41 Tests

SECOND TEST: Melboure (December 30-January 3 1961)

Richie Benaud won the toss and elected to bat, thus giving Australia the best of a wicket that became affected by rain. Ken Mackay was top scorer with 74 runs in a solid total of 348. Tail-ender Johnny Martin marked his Test debut with a well-struck 55. Frank Misson, a right-arm fast-medium bowler from New South Wales, was also making his bow for Australia and got off to a memorable start by having Conrad Hunte caught off his second ball. West Indies lost their first two wickets for just one run and only Seymour Nurse (70) and Rohan Kanhai (84) reached double figures in a total of 181. Alan Davidson was again the main des-troyer, taking 6 for 53. Benaud enforced the follow-on and a century by Hunte (110) and a contribution of 75 from Gerry Alexander saved West Indies from an innings defeat. Joe Solomon was out in an unusual way when his cap fell on his wicket as he played a defensive shot against the bowling of Benaud. Martin's debut became even more remarkable when he claimed the wickets of Kanhai, Sobers and Worrell in four balls. For skipper Worrell it was his second duck of the match. Needing just 67 runs for victory, Australia lost three wickets before Bobby Simpson and Les Favell saw them home safely. Rain had ended play just after lunch on the second day, but Australia still managed to win with a day to spare. **RESULT: Australia (348 and 70 for 3) beat West Indies (181 and 233) by 7 wickets.**

THIRD TEST: Sydney (January 13-18)

Lance Gibbs replaced Ramadhin and proved himself a more than worthy successor by helping to bowl West Indies to a convincing victory by 222 runs. Gary Sobers set the tourists on the road to their win with a superb innings of 168 on the first day. Australia were looking set to get within reach of the West Indies first innings total of 339 when Gibbs took the wickets of Mackay, Martin and Grout in four balls. Norm O'Neill (71) was again their top scorer in a reply of 202. Gerry Alexander scored his one and only first-class century and Frank Worrell weighed in with 82 as West Indies amassed 326 runs in their second innings. The pitch started to take spin and Gibbs (5-66), Alf Valentine (4-86) and Sobers (1-38) bowled out the Australians for 241 after a bright stand between Neil Harvey (85) and O'Neill (70). Of the late-order batsman only Benaud (24) offered any resistance and the match was all over and the series level before lunch on the fifth day. **RESULT: West Indies (339 and 326) beat Australia (202 and 241) by 222 runs.**

65

FOURTH TEST: Adelaide (January 27-February 1)

There was another heart-in-the-mouth finish to this Test that featured a procession of outstanding performances. Rohan Kanhai became the first West Indian to score a century in each innings of a Test in Australia as the tourists rattled up totals of 393 and 432 for 6 declared against an attack weakened by the absence of the unwell Davidson. Kanhai scored his first 100 in 126 minutes and his second in 150 minutes. In each innings he fell to Richie Benaud, and on the second occasion he became the Aussie captain's 200th victim in Test cricket. Gerry Alexander continued his excellent form with the bat by scoring 63 not out and 83 not out, and Worrell contributed 71 and 53. Australia's first innings was decimated by Gibbs who completed a hat-trick by dismissing Grout, Mackay and Misson after McDonald (71), Simpson (85), Burge (45) and Benaud (77) had produced solid knocks. It all seemed over for Australia when, needing a colossal 460 to win, they lost nine wickets for 207 runs. But in one of the most courageous last-wicket stands of all time Mackay and Kline defied a battery of West Indian bowlers in a partnership that survived the final 100 minutes of yet another amazing match. **RESULT: Match drawn. West Indies 393 and 432 for 6 dec., Australia 366 and 273 for 9.**

FIFTH TEST: Melbourne (February 10-15)

This final Test of a never-to-be-forgotten series lived up to the standards of excellence and excitement of the previous matches. Richie Benaud won the toss and boldly put the West Indians in to bat. Sobers was top scorer with 64 in a total of 292. Sobers then took the ball and bowled unchanged for 41 eight-ball overs, claiming 5 for 120 as Australia built a first innings score of 356 on a foundation of 146 runs by openers Bobby Simpson (75) and Colin McDonald (71). Conrad Hunte (52) and Gerry Alexander (73) stopped a total collapse of the West Indies batting against the pace and penetration of fit-again Alan Davidson, who took 5 for 84 in a match in which he completed the rare double of 1,000 Test runs and 100 Test wickets. Australia, needing 278, were given another flying send-off by Bobby Simpson (92), and O'Neill (48) and Burge (53) supported him with some powerful stroke play. They appeared to be in sight of victory in the match and the series at 254 for 7 on the fifth day of this six-day Test when there was yet another of those dramatic moments to which these so evenly balanced teams had become accustomed. A bail was dislodged following a ball from Valentine that was swept for two by Wally

66

Grout. The umpires decided after a long discussion that the bail had not been knocked off by the ball. In the same over, true sportsman Grout deliberately surrendered his wicket with a skied catch before ninth wicket partners Mackay and Martin scrambled a bye for victory in the Test and the rubber. The vast crowd swarmed on to the Melbourne pitch at the end and their chanted praise was as much for the vanquished West Indians as for the victorious Aussies after a series that raised world interest in cricket to new heights. **RESULT: Australia (356 and 258 for 8) beat West Indies (292 and 321) by 2 wickets.**

THE CAPTAIN

Richie Benaud was a phenomenally successful captain of Australia as well as being a leg spinner of the highest quality. It was his tactical genius that was a major reason for the Aussies winning four successive series under his inspiring leadership – against England twice, West Indies and Pakistan. The son of an Australian first-grade player who once took 20 wickets in a match, Richie combined a career in journalism with his cricket and when he finished playing it was a natural transition for him to become the television 'Voice of Cricket' both in Australia and England, his perceptive comments always capturing the state of play and revealing his total grasp of the game.

It was clear that Benaud was destined to be an outstanding cricketer from his schooldays, and he made his debut for New South Wales at the age of eighteen. Within three years he was in the Test team, selected as much for his batting as his bowling. He was an enterprising right-handed batsman who could turn a match with his late-order hitting. Nobody who saw his performance against T.N.Pearce's X1 in the traditional match at the Scarborough Festival in 1953 will forget the power in his shots. He struck 11 sixes and 9 fours on the way to a whirlwind 135.

As a bowler, he had exceptional control and accuracy, and he could outwit even the greatest batsmen on any wicket that offered him the slightest encouragement. English cricket followers rarely saw him at his best with the ball because he was more effective on the hard wickets overseas. He not only preached but practised the old maxim that practice makes perfect. Even when at his peak he would spend hours in the nets striving to improve his line, length and flight. His finest bowling display in England came on the final day of the Old Trafford Test of 1961. England were seemingly coasting to victory with just over 100 runs needed and nine second innings wickets standing when Benaud turned the match upside down by taking five wickets for 12 in just 25 balls. He

67

finished with figures of 6 for 70, a spell that lifted Australia to victory by 54 runs and clinched the retention of the Ashes.

He was a brilliant close fielder, though his effectiveness was curtailed late in his career by a recurring shoulder injury that eventually forced his retirement after he had taken a then record 248 Test wickets for Australia. Richie was also a recordbreaker in State cricket, taking 266 wickets in 73 matches for New South Wales. As good as he was as an all-round player, he will be best remembered for his captaincy that was always fiercely competitive but never unsporting. *Test record:* 63 Tests, 2,201 runs (average: 24.45), 3 centuries, 248 wickets (27.03), 65 catches. Captain in 28 Tests (12 wins, 4 defeats, 11 draws, 1 tie).

TOM GRAVENEY: 'Richie's great ability as a captain is best gauged by the fact that he took an ordinary Australian team and shaped it into a winning side. The squad he brought to England in 1961 shortly after the stirring series against the West Indies was in my opinion one of the weakest ever to tour here, yet they retained the Ashes because of Richie's bold and imaginative leadership. He was a marvellous motivator who was able to make players under him perform to the absolute peak of their form.

There has never been a captain to match him for an attacking outlook, and when Frank Worrell made a bold challenge for the 1960-61 series to be open and adventurous he found in Benaud a skipper ready to meet him more than halfway. I had a personal experience of Richie's tactical genius during England's 1958-59 tour. I was just getting my innings together in the fourth Test at Adelaide when he held up play while he moved the short leg round a couple of yards. It interrupted my flow because I was forced to wonder why he had done it and whether I should be expecting a new direction from the bowler. This was exactly the reaction that Richie had wanted. There was no reason for the move other than to apply psychological pressure. He was a master at upsetting the concentration of batsmen and reaching their subconscious.

As a leg-spinner Benaud was in a class of his own. He was not a great spinner of the ball in the mould of, say, Bruce Dooland or Doug Wright. But he could turn it enough to cause problems. It was his control of the ball that was his greatest asset. As well as the leg-break, he could release a googlie, the top-spinner and a 'flipper' that would baffle even the finest batsmen. Unlike most back-of-the-hand bowlers, he was rarely expensive and did not try to buy his wickets. He could close a game up like a left-hander, dropping the ball on a length and forcing batsmen on to the defensive. His target was usually the middle or off stump, but I remember him getting me out in the 1958-59 Melbourne Test by attacking my leg stump. He bowled me two half-volleys, the first of which I drove hard to Colin McDonald at mid-on. The second was just a fraction slower, and I was committed to my stroke before I spotted it. McDonald held the catch and the critics put it down to another casual shot by Graveney. They did not seem to notice the crafty part that Benaud had played in my dismissal. With all his great knowledge of the game, Richie was never too big to ask for advice and opinions from his senior colleagues and he used to lean on the experience of that super player Neil Harvey. That's something all the great captains have in common – the ability to listen, learn and then act. Richie was arguably the greatest of all post-war Test captains, particularly when you bear in mind that he got some outstanding results with teams under him that would not bear comparison with the finest in Australian cricket history. It was his positive, attack-minded leadership that made all the difference.'

THE PLAYERS

COLIN McDONALD
Born: November 17, 1928.
Test record: 47 Tests, 3,107 runs (average: 39.32)
5 centuries, 14 catches.
Colin McDonald was a capable right-handed opening batsman with a distinctive short backlift. A regular choice for Autralia throughout the 1950s, he had sound technique and was exceptionally strong off his back foot and an excellent player of swing bowling. McDonald possessed true fighting spirit and produced many of his best innings when Australia were in a backs-to-the-wall situation. In 1956, when Jim Laker took his 19 wickets at Old Trafford, McDonald was the only batsman to offer any real resistance, scoring 32 and 89. It was his opening stand of 137 with Jim Burke in the Lord's Test that set Australia on the way to their one victory of the 1956 tour. His last series was the memorable one against the West Indies in 1960-61 during which he had to face some ferocious new ball bowling from Wes Hall. McDonald managed to amass 357 runs during the series, including an invaluable knock of 91 in the decisive final Test. He was a successful Sheffield Shield player for Victoria and captained the State from 1958 to 1963 in succession to Ian Johnson. He twice scored double centuries in Shield matches. Following his retirement he went into a new line of sport as an official with the Australian Lawn Tennis Association.

BOBBY SIMPSON
Born: February 3, 1936.
Test Record: 62 Tests, 4,869 runs (average: 46.81)
10 centuries, 71 wickets (average: 42.26), 110 catches.

Bobby Simpson was an extremely gifted all-round cricketer who mastered every department of the game. He was a prolific run-maker as a right-handed opening or middle-order batsman who was suspect only against the very fastest bowlers. He had the technique and temperament to put together a procession of victory-building innings for Australia. He would start his innings cautiously but when he was established at the crease, he could be as exciting as any batsman in the world, using his quick footwork and wide array of strokes to push the score along. As well as being a more-than-useful leg-spin bowler, Simpson can claim to have been one of the greatest slip-fielders of all time. He had lightning-quick reflexes and it was rare indeed for a chance to go begging if the ball was anything like catchable and within his reach. He captained Australia 39 times over two periods, returning to the Test arena as a world-wise veteran to supervise the rebuilding of a new team following the Kerry Packer revolution that knocked great holes in the Australian Test squad. His finest performances for Australia came in harness with his left-handed opening partner Bill Lawry, who was his successor as captain the first time around. His most memorable innings in England was his marathon 311 in the Old Trafford Test on the 1964 tour. The following year in the West Indies he and Lawry shared a record opening stand of 382 in the Bridgetown Test. Simpson's contribution was 201. As a captain, he tended to put caution before confidence but he had the respect of his players and opponents alike for the firm but fair way in which he approached the game he served with such distinction.

NEIL HARVEY
Born: October 8, 1928.
Test record: 6,149 runs (average: 48.42)
21 centuries, 64 catches.

Neil Harvey was the left-handed master who during a 15-year Test career lit up the cricket stage with the sunshine of his style. Tom Graveney says that it was an absolute pleasure to watch him in action even when in the field chasing his shots to the boundary. Harvey was the Fred Astaire of cricket, with marvellous footwork ensuring that he was always in the right position at the right time. He could be vulnerable outside the off stump early in his innings but, once he was in full flow, it was almost impossible to find the bowlers and the field to check him. Harvey was also one of the most exciting fielders the game of cricket has seen. It was almost worth the admission money just to see him swooping at cover point and returning a smooth and deadly accurate throw. He played in a then record 79 Tests for Australia between 1948 and 1963 and his compilation of runs was second only to the run mountain created by the untouchable Don Bradman. His highest Test score was 205 against the South African tourists in Melbourne in 1952-53, a match in which he finished on the losing side. He played in 37 Tests against England and included six centuries in his 2,416 runs. The only time he failed to make an impressive impact was on the 1956 tour when he managed to collect his only pair in Test cricket during the 'Laker Match' at Old Trafford. Yet even when out of touch on that tour he managed to put together an innings of 69 in the Headingley Test that revealed his great craftsmanship. It was the highest score in either innings for Australia in a match in which most of his colleagues could hardly get their bat to the ball. Tom Graveney is among those who consider that his greatest innings was a battling, undefeated 92 out of a total of 184 in Melbourne in 1954-55 when Frank Tyson and Brian Statham were at their most lethal.

NORMAN O'NEILL
Born: February 19, 1937.
Test record: 42 Tests, 2,779 runs (average: 45.55)
6 centuries, 17 wickets (average: 39.23), 21 catches.

Norm O'Neill was a talented right-handed attacking batsman who never quite reached the astronomical heights expected of him in the arena of international cricket. He was heralded as the 'new Don Bradman' when he burst into first-class cricket at the age of eighteen, but that was a label that weighed on him at times like a sack of cement. He was an exceptionally strong back foot player who looked invincible when he was settled at the wicket, but he was an extremely nervous starter who often got himself dismissed early in his innings playing a rash stroke. His fielding in the deep or in the covers was always of the highest standard, and he was also a fair leg-spin bowler who had the knack of breaking big partnerships. He averaged 51.12 through his 12-year career before a recurring knee injury forced his retirement. It was a run average that showed he was a player of class and consistency, yet because of his earlier build-up as the 'new Bradman' he was never quite able to establish himself as one of the greats, despite having all the necessary attributes apart from the right early-innings temperament. He will never forget his first Test century because it came in the historic tied Test in 1960-61 when his 181 in the Australian first innings helped put the magic into the match.

LES FAVELL
Born: October 6, 1929. Died 1987.
Test record: 19 Tests, 757 runs (average: 27.03)
1 century, 9 catches.

A powerful right-handed opening batsman, Les Favell brought strength to the middle-order for most of the 1960-61 series against West Indies. He was a stocky, muscular batsman who liked to attack the bowling right from the start of his innings. Included in his armoury was a flashing hook shot that he would introduce at the first opportunity. He was capable of wrecking a bowling attack and spreading a field in an explosive burst of aggression, but his carefree batting style often led to an early dismissal from a reckless stroke. Les, who sadly died of cancer in 1987,was a heavy scorer throughout his career with South Australia, amassing 12,379 runs but he failed to gather runs consistently at Test level. His one Test century came against India in Madras in 1959-60, an innings that helped lay the foundation to victory by an innings and 55 runs. He captained Australia on a tour of New Zealand and was a respected skipper of South Australia for whom he later became an administrator. His commentaries on ABC Radio were always authoritative.

KEN MACKAY
Born: October 24, 1941. *Died:* June 13, 1982.
Test record: 37 Tests, 1,507 runs (average: 33.48)
50 wickets (average: 34.42), 17 catches.

One of the most frustrating and discouraging sights for a fielding side in a Test match was the appearance of Ken 'Slasher' Mackay at the wicket. He was a consistent all-round cricketer who is best remembered for his patient, often plodding left-handed batting that time and again rescued Australia from defeat. He was also a right-arm medium-pace change bowler who took 50 Test wickets, but was mainly used as a containing bowler. His most successful bowling performance came against India in Dacca in 1959-60 when he took 6 for 42 on a matting wicket to lift Australia to victory by eight wickets. Mackay used to chew gum incessantly while giving total concentration to the defence of his wicket, and he was in the Trevor Bailey league when it came to stubborness under fire. His single-minded composure was not confined to the Test arena. He once took 15 minutes short of 10 hours scoring a career-best 223 for Queensland against Victoria. In all during his 17-year career he scored 10,823 runs at an average 43.64 – and a lot of them came at a quick rate of knots despite his reputation as a hoarder rather than a scorer of runs. More than half his runs plus 122 wickets were collected in 100 Sheffield Shield matches.

ALAN DAVIDSON
Born: June 14, 1929.
Test record: 44 Tests, 1,328 runs (average: 24.59)
186 wickets (average: 20.53), 42 catches.

Alan Davidson was a truly world-class all-rounder, and a key member of the Australian side over a span of 44 Tests. Early in his career he was a slow left-arm spinner before becoming possibly the greatest left-arm new ball bowler in the history of cricket. He could really whip up a terrific pace, but he usually preferred to bowl just within himself so that he could keep total control over the ball. 'Davo' perfected the art of making the ball move late in the air and off the pitch in either direction, and was expert at tempting batsmen to play at balls outside the off-stump. They would invariably get a snick and present a catch to a close fielder. His best bowling return in Test cricket was 7 for 93 against India in Kanpur in 1959-60, and in 25 Tests against England he took 84 wickets and scored 750 runs. He was an adventurous, hard-hitting left-handed batsman who played many vital innings for his country although he never managed a Test century. He could defend with skill and patience when the situation called for caution, and he was a selfless team player who always put the interests of the team above his own. 'Davo' was also an outstanding fielder, who could throw with great accuracy from the deep and his spectacular catching close to the wicket earned him the nickname 'Claws'. Once a bank clerk, he moved up through the ranks to manager and then director, and also became President of the New South Wales Cricket Association that he always served so well as a player.

WALLY GROUT
Born: March 30, 1927. *Died:* November 9, 1968.
Test record: 51 Tests, 890 runs (average: 15.08)
163 catches, 24 stumpings.

No wicket keeper had safer hands than Wally Grout. He was a marvellous opponent, who was always sporting and cheerful while – like all Aussies – retaining a steely will to win. He was an alert and nimble keeper with rapid reflexes and great powers of concentration. Batsmen always had to think twice about playing a fine leg-glance with Wally behind the stumps, because he was always liable to launch himself into a spectacular dive to make an 'impossible' catch. He was also a very capable batsman who often opened the innings for Queensland, although he scored only three half-centuries for his country. Twice in Test matches he was responsible for eight dismissals. His most memorable match came against South Africa in Johannesburg in 1957-58 when he pouched six catches in an innings and shared with Richie Benaud an eighth wicket stand of 89. Playing for Queensland against Western Australia at Brisbane in 1959-60, he held a world-record eight catches in an innings.

JOHNNY MARTIN
Born: July 28, 1931.
Test record: 8 Tests, 214 runs (average: 17.83)
17 wickets (average: 48.94), 5 catches.
Johnny Martin was a left arm spin bowler who was a prolific wicket taker in Australian State cricket but failed to make a lasting impact at Test level. He bowled a mixture of off-breaks and googlies and looked a high-class bowler when he got the ball on the right length and line. He was, however, inclined to inconsistency and after his initial success in his first series against the West Indies in 1960-61 he played in only a handful of Tests. He was also a useful and aggressive right-handed late-order batsman and a good fielder. His enthusiasm and endeavour made him a favourite with Colne in the Lancashire League.

FRANK MISSON
Born: November 19, 1938.
Test record: 5 Tests, 38 runs (average: 19.00)
16 wickets (average: 38.50), 6 catches.
Frank Misson was one of a procession of fast-medium bowlers tried by the Australian selectors in their search for successors to Lindwall and Miller, but he did not have the necessary penetrative powers to clinch a regular Test place. He was accurate with his deliveries and had great stamina which made him more suited to the role of stock bowler than strike bowler. Misson, who took Conrad Hunte's wicket with his second ball in Test cricket, played in the first two Tests against England on the 1961 tour but his bowling lacked vital zip on English wickets.

THEY ALSO SERVED

PETER BURGE
Born: May 17, 1932.
Test record: 42 Tests, 2,290 runs (average: 38.16)
4 centuries, 23 catches.
Peter Burge was, unlike most Australian batsmen, happiest on his front foot. He seemed to save his finest performances for Test matches against England. His knocks of 181 at The Oval in 1961 and 160 at Headingley in 1964 are remembered as two of the most enterprising innings against England during the '60s. Burge

74

was encouraged to be an adventurous cricketer from an early age by his father, who managed the Australian team with which Peter made his first Test tour of the West Indies in 1955. While he was always on the look out for quick runs, the Queenslander had a sound defence and could patiently lay the foundation to an innings before cutting loose with a fusilade of shots that included a particularly potent hook. A tall man who put on a lot of weight late in his career, he became known as 'Burge the Bulge' in the Queensland State where he remains a respected and influential member of the cricket scene.

DESMOND HOARE
Born: October 19, 1934.
Test record: 1 Test. 35 runs, 2 catches
2 wickets for 156 runs off 29 overs.

He took more than 200 wickets for Western Australia in a career that spanned 11 years from 1955. His one and only Test appearance was in the drawn fourth match of the 1960-61 series against the West Indies at the Adelaide Oval. Standing in for the unwell Alan Davidson, he made a startling beginning to his short-lived Test career when he trapped Conrad Hunte lbw in his second over. He later had Frank Worrell caught by Misson after the West Indies skipper had stroked 71 runs in a hard-hitting partnership with Rohan Kanhai. After scoring 35 valuable runs, Hoare's hopes of establishing himself in the Test team disappeared in the second innings when he has hammered for 88 runs in 13 overs without the consolation of a wicket.

IAN MECKIFF
Born: January 6, 1935.
Test record: 18 Tests. 154 runs (average 11.84)
45 wickets (31.62), 9 catches

Ian Meckiff's explosive career as a left-arm fast bowler ended under a cloud of controversy when he was called for throwing four times in his first over of the 1963-64 Brisbane Test against South Africa. Meckiff, taken off by skipper Richie Benaud, announced after the match that he would never play first-class cricket again. He had been dogged by accusations of throwing his faster ball throughout his headline-hitting Test career. Until this abrupt finish to his playing days at the age of 28, Meckiff had been a main strike bowler for Victoria and had taken 269 wickets at an average 23.35. There had been charges from the England players during the 1958-59 series that both Meckiff and his giant partner Gordon Rorke occasionally threw the ball. It was four years later when Australian umpire Colin Egar brought it all to a head by his decision to no ball the second, third, fifth and ninth balls of what proved to be Meckiff's final over in first-class cricket.

LINDSAY KLINE
Born: September 29, 1934.
Test record: 13 Tests. 58 runs (average: 8.28)
34 wickets (22.82), 9 catches.

For all his skill as a left-arm off-break and googly bowler, Lindsay Kline will always have his name first associated with his performance with the bat in the fourth Test of the 1960-61 series against the West Indies. With a career average of less than 10, he was something of a rabbit as a batsman. But he managed to defy the West Indies attack for 100 minutes in a last-wicket partnership with Ken Mackay that saved the match for Australia. Kline's undefeated contribution to a stand of 66 was just 15 runs during a partnership when it was not scoring that mattered so much as surviving. The highlight of his Test career as a bowler came in his second match against South Africa at Cape Town in 1957-58. He finished the match and clinched an innings victory for Australia by performing a hat-trick, taking the wickets of Eddie Fuller, Hugh Tayfield and Neil Adcock. He topped the averages in that series in South Africa with 15 wickets (16.33). His best bowling return in the Test arena was 7 for 75 against Pakistan in Lahore in 1959-60.

THE TOM GRAVENEY ASSESSMENT

It is the two captains, Richie Benaud and Frank Worrell, who must take the credit for the 1960-61 series becoming one of the greatest of all classics in cricket history. I don't believe England could have been involved in such an open and adventurous series because, by tradition, we breed our captains with a defensive streak buried just beneath the surface. This is not a criticism of England captains, rather a comment on the way we tend to approach our cricket. Caution is often our watchword, and it would take quite a revolution to introduce the sort of carefree approach of the West Indians. We would not have been prepared to meet Worrell's challenge for cricket combat in which all-out attack was the order of the day from first ball to last. The purists will point out how many tactical mistakes both Australia and West Indies made during each of the Tests, and I am sure an England captain – with winning rather than entertaining upper-most in mind – would have closed the games down the moment any batsmen looked ready to break loose.

Richie Benaud is one of the few Aussie captains who would have been prepared to take up Worrell's challenge, because generally speaking Aussie skippers – deep down – are just as defensive-minded as their English counterparts. Man for man, I reckon the West Indians were the superior side but Benaud was able to lift his players to new peaks with his dynamic leadership. He was fortunate in having Alan Davidson at his best in four of the Tests. Despite missing one of the Tests, he took 33 West Indian wickets and as if that wasn't enough of a contribution he finished the series with batting average of 30. I used to look on 'Davo' as the healthiest hypochondriac in the game. He always seemed to be suffering from injury or illness and just when he had your sympathy he would suddenly be there at the wicket zipping the ball past you at a tremendous rate of knots.

To mark their triumph, Australia became the first holders of the Frank Worrell Trophy which was presented by the Australian Board of Control for perpetual competition between the two nations. It was named as an affectionate tribute to Worrell's contribution to a series that gave Australian cricket a massive boost. But it takes two to tango and it was everybody's good fortune that Richie Benaud was in the mood for dancing!

There were no losers in this series, and the biggest winner of all was the game of cricket because Australia and West Indies showed the way the game could and should be played.

Frank Worrell's West Indies, 1963

THE SQUAD:

Conrad Hunte (5)	Gary Sobers (5)	Wes Hall (5)
Joey Carew (2)	Joe Solomon (3)	Charlie Griffith (5)
Rohan Kanhai (5)	Frank Worrell (5)	Lance Gibbs (5)
Basil Butcher (5)	Deryck Murray (5)	Easton McMorris (2)
	Willie Rodriguez (1)	

SCOREBOARD: 5 Tests, 3 wins, 1 defeat, 1 draw

Figures in brackets indicate the number of Test match appearances

---

BACKGROUND

West Indies followed their unforgettable series in Australia with a 5-0 whitewash of India in the Caribbean in 1962, and by the time of the 1963 tour to England Frank Worrell had pieced together a side that was brimming over with all-round skill and strength. The bowling attack was made twice as penetrative by the pairing of Wes Hall with Charlie Griffith, whose fastest deliveries were reckoned to be as quick as anything ever seen on a cricket field. Lance Gibbs was now firmly installed as the first-choice spinner, and the incomparable Gary Sobers was in support with his selection of three left-arm bowling styles. Deryck Murray, a 20-year-old college student from Trinidad, had emerged as a wicket keeper of enormous promise, and the batting line-up bulged with the power and class of players like Sobers, Conrad Hunte, Rohan Kanhai, Seymour Nurse and the exciting newcomer to English wickets, Basil Butcher.

The one glaring weakness was the lack of an established and effective opening partnership, but such was the strength in depth that Worrell had no real cause for concern. The West Indies skipper was determined to mark his final tour with an exhibition of cricket that would, as in Australia two years earlier, have the emphasis on attacking flair and style. At 38, he was into the

78

closing stages of his glittering career, but despite knees that were feeling the strain he remained an influential batsman and he could still bowl a tidy over. But his biggest influence was as a captain who had the total respect and affection of every one of his players, and each of them was committed to giving him a winning finale.

TOM GRAVENEY: 'The two men who really gave West Indies a decisive edge over England were new ball partners Wes Hall and Charlie Griffith. I vividly recall playing against them at the start of the tour when they were operating together for the first time in England. They rushed out the Worcestershire team for a little over a hundred. I managed to score 69. I was hoping to get the chance to pit my skills against them in the Test series, but the selectors seemed to have written me off. It was three years later in 1966 when I was recalled to the England team to face Hall and Griffith and I was able to accumulate quite a few runs against them, including a couple of centuries. But in that summer of '63 I would say they were as hostile as any pair of pacemen in the history of the game.

It's worth recording that Hall and Griffith were operating in the pre-helmet days, and if ever a batsman needed protection it was when these two were firing the ball down at something approaching 100 miles per hour. Wes, one of the nicest people you could wish to meet off the pitch, was a demon of a bowler who had a classical action and *Pace Like Fire* – which was the apt title of his autobiography. Charlie Griffith was nothing like as graceful as Hall, but his bouncers and yorkers were just about the most dangerous balls I have ever seen delivered. Throughout much of his career Charlie was hounded by the controversy as to whether or not he threw the ball. He certainly had a suspect action when releasing his fastest delivery that used to come through at you at lightning speed. He unnerved one or two of England's established batsmen, and several – including Ken Barrington and Ted Dexter – publicly pointed the finger of suspicion at his bowling action. Charlie was the centre of so much criticism during the series that he changed from being a big, amiable giant to a morose and moody individual, which was right against the cheerful, sporting image that Frank Worrell and his wonders projected throughout a tour when they touched tremendous peaks of achievement. They got close to reproducing the thrills and excitement of their memorable tour to Australia in 1960-61, and once again they put a big smile on the face of cricket. Mind you, they didn't leave the England cricketers with too much to smile about! They gave us a fair old hiding.'

THE OPPOSITION

Ted Dexter was skipper of an uninspired England team that was into an unproductive phase following the premature retirement of the majestic Peter May. The selectors were leaning too heavily on the pace of Fred Trueman and a procession of out-of-form batsmen to hold any real hope of mastering one of the strongest sides ever to tour England. It was felt that Colin Cowdrey would be a key man, but any hopes England had of winning the series virtually disappeared when he broke an arm while facing the fearsome Hall in the second Test. Trueman had raised English hopes in May when playing for Yorkshire against the tourists. He had a match analysis of 10 for 81 and was the man mainly responsible for West Indies being beaten by 111 runs. But it was a West Indies team missing Hall, Hunte and Gibbs, all of whom were to play major roles in the Test series.

THE TEST MATCHES
FIRST TEST: Old Trafford (June 6-10)

Skipper Worrell won the toss and that proved crucial. West Indies were able to bat first on a wicket that started to break up as early as the second day. Opener Conrad Hunte laid the foundation to a colossal total with a patiently compiled 182 not out, taking eight hours over his masterpiece of an innings while Kanhai (90), Sobers (64) and Worrell (74 not out) made a cavalier dash for runs before a declaration at 501 for 6. England, with Surrey trio Micky Stewart, John Edrich and Ken Barrington batting 1-2-3, failed to save the follow-on and were finally beaten by 10 wickets. In fact they were just one run off an innings defeat. It was Lance Gibbs who did the damage on a pitch that took spin from the third day. He finished with 5 for 59 in the first innings and 6 for 98 in the second. Only Ted Dexter (73 in the first innings) and Micky Stewart (87 in the second innings) got above 40 for England. It was the first victory by West Indies in a Test at Old Trafford. **RESULT: West Indies (501 for 6 declared and 1-0) beat England (205 and 296) by 10 wickets.)**

SECOND TEST: Lord's (June 20-25)

This match provided a finish almost on a par with the tied Melbourne Test for excitement and drama. Any one of four results was possible as Wes Hall prepared to bowl the last over of the match! England started this last over with eight wickets down

80

and needing eight runs to win. Tail-enders Derek Shackleton and David Allen were at the wicket while Colin Cowdrey, his left arm in plaster after being hit by a ball from Hall when 19, sat padded up in the pavilion ready to resume his innings in dire emergency. England scored singles off the second and third balls. Three balls left, six runs needed. Shackleton missed the fourth ball but set off down the pitch in a wild charge for a bye. Wicket keeper Murray fielded the ball and shied at the stumps...and missed. Worrell coolly collected the ball and dashed to the far end of the pitch with the ball in his hand. It was a race between the veteran West Indies skipper and Shackleton, and Worrell won by a short head as he knocked the bails off to run Shack out. Two balls left, six runs needed...and coming to the non-striker's end was the wounded Cowdrey. He planned if necessary to bat one-handed, but David Allen played the last two balls with a defensive straight bat to clinch just about the most exciting drawn result ever witnessed in a Test match.

There were many memorable moments in the build-up to this breath-taking finale. Wes Hall bowled unchanged throughout the three hours 20 minutes of play that were possible on a rain-hit final day. He unleashed 40 overs flat out and finished with 4 for 93. Hunte had given the match an incredible send-off by dispatching Freddie Trueman's first three balls to the boundary for three fours. But Trueman refused to admit defeat and took 6 for 100 in the first innings and finished with match figures of 11 for 152. Shackleton ended West Indies' first innings by snatching three wickets in four balls. When England replied, Ted Dexter played one of the finest innings of his career to stop Hall and Griffith (5-91) in their tracks. He sizzled to 70 off 73 balls before Sobers brought one back to trap him lbw. Ken Barrington battled to 80 and Freddie Titmus was not out 52 in England's total of 297. Trueman and Shackleton (4-72) looked set to run through the West Indies batting in their second innings until Basil Butcher applied the brake and hammered 133 out of a total of 229, including two sixes and 17 fours in his battery of runs.

Barrington (70) and then the unbelieveably brave Brian Close (60) – taking blows from Hall and Griffith on the body without flinching – pulled England back into the game with a victory chance. This followed a collapse to 31 for 3 and then the retire-ment of Cowdrey after he had failed to get out of the way of a wickedly rising ball from Hall. Millions of television viewers were tuned into the last hour of play, and the final heart-stopping over was followed by a crowd invasion of the pitch, with hundreds of spectators saluting one of the finest matches ever played at the headquarters of cricket.

THIRD TEST: Edgbaston (July 4-9)

On a rain-affected pitch, Fred Trueman showed that anything Hall and Griffith could do he could do equally well. He bowled England to victory by 217 runs with a match haul of 12 wickets for 119, a record for any bowler in a Test at Birmingham. His last six wickets were taken in a 24-ball spell which cost him just one scoring stroke for four by Lance Gibbs as the West Indies collapsed to a second innings total of 91. Only Brian Close (55) topped the half-century for either side in the first innings. Jerry Carew (40) was top scorer for the West Indies whose batsmen all struggled against the pace of Trueman and the swing of Shackleton and Dexter. England recovered from 69 for 4 in their second innings to 278 for 9 declared, thanks mainly to a gritty debut performance by Phil Sharpe (85 not out) who shared solid stands with Dexter (57) and Tony Lock (56). Rohan Kanhai (38) was top scorer for the West Indies in a second innings that became a nightmare on a pitch that was tailormade for Trueman's devastating seam bowling. **RESULT: England (216 and 278) beat the West Indies (186 and 91) by 217 runs.**

FOURTH TEST: Headingley (July 25-29)

Any doubts that West Indies were the superior side were wiped away at Headingley. The big guns came out – Sobers (102), Kanhai (92), Joe Solomon (62) – as they amassed 397 in their first innings. Then Charlie Griffith was let off the leash and he swept through England's batting, taking 6 for 36 in 21 deadly overs. For the first time there was open debate about his action, and allegations that he threw his faster ball brought a cloud of controversy over the rest of his career. Butcher (78), Sobers (58) and Kanhai (44) pushed the West Indies second innings total up to 229 and their lead to a massive 453. Only Brian Close (56) and wicket keeper Jim Parks (53) managed more than 50 as Griffith (3-45), Gibbs (4-76) and Sobers (3-90) combined to bowl England out for 231 and to sew the game up just after lunch on the fourth day. **RESULT: West Indies (397 and 229) beat England (229 and 231) by 221 runs.**

FIFTH TEST: The Oval (August 22-26)

West Indies won the Wisden Trophy by three Tests to one with an emphatic eight wicket victory as their supporters provided a carnival atmosphere at The Oval. It was the batting of Conrad Hunte and the bowling of Charlie Griffth that proved the match-winning factors for Frank Worrell's exciting team. England batted first and were all out for 275 against some hostile bowling from Griffith who claimed 6 wickets for 71 and was ticked off by the umpire for letting go too many bouncers. Yorkshiremen Phil Sharpe (63) and Brian Close (46) were again the most productive of England's batsmen. Conrad Hunte (80) and Basil Butcher (53) put some beef into the West Indies reply but Trueman (3-65) and Statham (3-68) combined to keep their total down to 246. Hall (4-39) and Griffith (3-66) were again a winning double act and Sobers (3-77) gave superb support to send England tumbling for 223 in their second innings despite another fighting display by Sharpe (83). The series ended as it started, with Conrad Hunte producing some delightful shots on his way to an unbeaten 108 that steered West Indies to a winning total of 255 for the loss of just two wickets against an England attack weakened by an injury to Trueman. Kanhai gave a sparkling exhibition of stroke play to bring victory in sight with 77 runs in 70 minutes. The Oval was alight with the sunshine of the Caribbean. **RESULT: West Indies (246 and 255 for 2) beat England (275 and 223) by 8 wickets.**

THE CAPTAIN

There has never been a more respected captain than Sir Frank Mortimer Maglinne Worrell, who was knighted in 1964 for his services to cricket. Even if he had never tossed a coin he would have been remembered and revered as one of the finest batsmen of all time, and also as a bowler of considerable talent. But it is as a captain that he has gone down in cricketing history as an all-time great.

Worrell was a man of pleasant personality who was quietly persuasive and won the loyalty and total respect of his players with leadership that owed as much to example as exhortation. Cricket in general and West Indies in particular owe him a debt for the way he approached the game, always demanding that his team play with style, sportsmanship and flair. For Worrell, the game came first – winning second. He more than anybody laid the foundation for the procession of great West Indian teams that have thrilled the world with their calypso cricket.

Captaincy of his country was a long time coming to him. The West Indian selectors did not turn to him as their first black overseas tour captain until one crisis after another had pushed them into a corner. They finally handed him the reins for the challenging 1960-61 tour of Australia, and the rest is history. He was thirty-six by then and preparing for retirement, but he vowed to carry on until he had completed the job of pointing West Indian cricket back in the right direction after the slump that followed their startling successes of the early '50s in which he played a prominent part as one of 'the three Ws'.

He had started his career as a slow left-arm bowler at the age of eighteen in 1942, making his debut for Barbados without ever having seen a first-class match. Barbados found out by accident that he had even more promise as a batsman. He was sent in as a nightwatchman in 1943 and after stroking his way to 64 not out was promoted to opener. In his first full season as a recognized batsman he scored an undefeated 308 while sharing a stand of 502 with John Goddard against Trinidad. Two years later he and Clyde Walcott shared another unbroken stand against Trinidad, this time putting on 574 runs. He was being groomed for Test honours and on a tour of India with a Commonwealth side in 1949-50 he averaged 97 in ten unofficial Test matches.

The peak of a succession of stunning performances in England during the 1950 tour was a magnificent innings of 261 in the Trent Bridge Test. He had by then stepped up from spin bowling to medium pace, and he could often make a new ball move as quickly as the fastest bowlers. Twice in a single innings in Test matches he took seven wickets. Like several of his team-mates, his form dipped in the mid-1950s but he brought some order back to the West Indies batting on the 1957 tour of England, and he almost single handedly rescued them from defeat in the Trent Bridge Test with an unbeaten 191.

He was past his playing pinnacle when handed the captaincy, but even in the veteran stages of his distinguished career he could still turn a match with a well-judged innings or with bowling that was not as fast as in his peak years but still deadly in its accuracy. The cricketing world acclaimed his knighthood following his retirement in 1964 and mourned his early passing from leukaemia three years later at the age of forty-two, just as he was starting to establish himself as a respected academic within the University of the West Indies where his specialist subject was sociology. *Test record:* 51 Tests, 3,860 runs (average: 49.48), 69 wickets (average: 38.72), 43 catches. Captain in 15 Tests (won 9, lost 3, drew 2, 1 tie).

TOM GRAVENEY: 'Frank Worrell's greatest achievement as captain was the way in which he managed to bring discipline to his team without in any way lessening the individual skills of his players. Generally speaking, West Indians can be a volatile lot and until Worrell was at last given the captaincy their team play was suffering because of a lack of togetherness when the pressure was on them. But Frank pulled them all together with his quiet, firm leadership. He moulded West Indies from a mixed-up gathering of Island individualists into a magnificent team. I cannot once remember seeing Frank looking flustered or with anything less than total control of the situation. Even when the Charlie Griffith throwing controversy was at its peak Frank kept the lid on what could have been a gigantic blow-up. He just quietly told Charlie to cool it when the umpires were gunning for him. Histrionics had no place in his life. He was like the Perry Como of cricket. He looked so relaxed at times you wondered if he was asleep at the crease, but a thundering shot off the next ball would quickly dispel that thought.

His mild manner and pleasant personality masked a grim determination to win matches, but never at all costs. He was a true sportsman who never once in his career attempted to win by any other means than fair. Frank's career lasted longer at the top than that of his plundering partners Everton Weekes and Clyde Walcott because he was technically superior to them. He used to play through the line in the way of orthodox English batsmen, and when his power started to desert him he still had the technique to accumulate big totals. I was fortunate when playing against Frank in that I often managed big scores, and when the England teams used to be announced in 1963 I was told that his first question used to be, "Is Graveney playing?" Well, nothing was a greater pleasure than for me to share the same field as this master of the game. Whether batting, bowling or fielding, he was an absolute joy to behold.'

THE PLAYERS

CONRAD HUNTE
Born: May 9, 1932.
Test record: 44 Tests, 3,245 runs (average: 45.06)
8 centuries, 2 wickets (average: 55), 16 catches.
Conrad Hunte provided the backbone for West Indian batting throughout the 1960s. He was, by nature, a talented attacking stroke-maker, but as he matured he tethered his instincts for adventure in the interests of the team. Conrad developed into a solid and dependable right-handed opening batsman with a preference for putting saftey first. The West Indies struggled to find a consistent opening partner for him and he was often left with the responsibility of seeing off the new ball on his own. He pefected a simple but effective batting technique based on stubborn defence and deft deflections and inch-perfect pushes to accumulate his runs. He was a particularly strong player off his

legs and the majority of his runs came through the mid-wicket area. He was also a fine close-in fielder and an occasional medium-pace bowler. Hunte made an impressive start to his Test career, scoring 142 runs in his debut innings against Pakistan in 1957-58, and in the third Test of the same series he scored 260 runs and shared a record partnership for West Indies of 446 for the second wicket with Gary Sobers, who went on to gather his world record innings of 365 not out. He collected eight Test match centuries and topped the West Indies batting averages on several tours, including the 1963 tour of England when he emerged as the matchwinner in the first and final Test matches. He was a deeply religious man who retired from cricket in 1967 to become a dedicated advocate of Moral Rearmament .

MICHAEL CAREW
Born: September 15, 1937.
Test record: 19 Tests, 1,127 runs (average: 34.15)
1 century, 8 wickets (average: 54.62), 13 catches.
Michael 'Joey' Carew was a talented left-handed opening batsman, who played with typical West Indian aggression and gusto. He operated mainly off the back foot and when timing the ball sweetly was a threat to any bowler in the world. He was, however, inclined to be inconsistent and was vulnerable outside the off stump, particularly in English conditions. He was at his best on hard, bouncy wickets as he proved on the 1968-69 West Indian tour of Australasia. He scored 90 runs against Australia in the second innings of the fourth Test at Adelaide and 64 in the next Test at Sydney, before compiling his only Test century against New Zealand at Auckland when he made 109. He was a competent fielder and an occasional change bowler. He continued to take a close interest in the game following his retirement, and he eventually became a West Indian Test selector.

ROHAN KANHAI
Born: December 26, 1935.
Test record: 79 Tests, 6,227 runs (average: 47.53)
15 centuries, 50 catches.
Rohan Kanhai was a wonderfully gifted right-handed batsman who was a permanent fixture in the West Indies side from 1957 to 1974. He scored runs heavily and consistently throughout his career and became a popular and well-respected cricketer all over the world. His batting was a mixture of natural West Indian flamboyance, intense concentration and patience and unorthodox, inventive stroke-making. His most famous shot was his off-balance sweep shot when, invariably, he would end up on his

back-side while the ball was on its way into the stands. There was no real weakness in his batting technique, although there was a question mark over his sometimes volatile temperament. He could on occasions seem almost disinterested at the wicket, but when he was giving the game his full attention there have been few to equal his all-round batting prowess. In 1958-59, he scored the first of his 15 Test centuries against India at Calcutta and carried on to lift his total to 256 runs, including 42 boundaries. In the same season in Pakistan, he scored a chanceless 217 in the third Test at Lahore. While in Australia in 1960-61 he became the first West Indian to score two centuries in the same Test match, striking 117 and 115 at Adelaide. Early in that tour he created an innings of 252 against Victoria that many onlookers rated the finest batting exhibition they had ever seen. He was only small of stature, but was a true giant of the game who was a prolific globetrotting runmaker for Guyana, Western Australia and Tasmania as well as becoming a key member of the Warwickshire side. Kanhai succeeded Gary Sobers as West Indies skipper, but he did not have the sort of personality and attitude suited to the demands and discipline of captaincy. He was too much of a free spirit who liked to do things his way, and that was too often the unorthodox way. He led West Indies in 13 Tests, of which they won just three.

BASIL BUTCHER
Born: September 3, 1933.
Test record: 44 Tests, 3,104 runs (average: 43.11)
7 centuries, 5 wickets (average: 18), 15 catches.
Basil Butcher was a reliable right-handed middle-order batsman who thrived in English conditions and made a habit of producing his best in Test matches against England. Unlike most Caribbean cricketers, he was not a spectacular stroke-maker but more a steady accumulator of runs. His greatest assets were his powers of concentration and patience. He established himself as a player of real class and courage in the 1963 Lord's Test when he contributed 133 to a West Indian total of 229, going in to bat after learning that his wife had suffered a miscarriage. He won a regular place in the West Indies team and his seven Test centuries were all put together in tense, backs-to-the-wall situations. In two more tours of England he garnered runs consistently, including his Test highest of 209 not out in the 1966 Trent Bridge encounter. Basil was a useful leg-break bowler who took 5 for 34 against England in 1968 at Port of Spain. He completed 31 first-class centuries in his 18-year career during which he became a popular Lancashire League cricketer.

GARY SOBERS

Born: July 28, 1936.
Test record: 93 Tests, 8,032 runs (average: 57.78)
26 centuries, 235 wickets (average: 34.03), 109 catches.

When Garfield St Aubrun Sobers made his Test debut as a raw
17-year-old slow left-arm bowler in 1954, it was soon obvious
that the West Indies had unearthed a diamond of a player, and
within just a few years he had developed into perhaps the greatest
cricketer of all-time. As a batsman, he was a marvellous big-
occasion player who produced a procession of outstanding performances in the Test arena. He was a master of invention who had
a sound technique and also that West Indian flair for being able to
improvise shots. In 1958, at the age of 21, Sobers scored the first
of his 26 Test centuries against Pakistan in Kingston, Jamaica.
Not satisfied with a century, he went on to amass a world record
365 not out and the message flashed around the cricket world that
here was a remarkable and magnificent cricketer.

Sobers was also without doubt one of the most versatile
bowlers in the history of cricket. When taking the new ball he
could unleash a delivery that was as fast as that of the quickest of
the front-line bowlers. His fast-medium seamers swung viciously
while keeping a perfect line and length. Or he could be a slow
left-arm bowler who was able to tie batsman down for long spells
or baffle them with wicked spin. Sobers was an adventurous
captain – perhaps too adventurous – and was always willing to
take a gamble to get a result out of a match. He captained the
West Indies in 39 Tests, winning nine of them and drawing 10.
Along with all his other gifts, he was also a superb fielder who
was exceptionally quick and safe close to the wicket. In the later
stages of his career he was hindered by a recurring knee injury
but could still conjure up an innings of breath-taking skill and
power.

His swashbuckling approach to cricket was captured in just
one historic over when he was playing for Notts against
Glamorgan at Somerset in 1968. He skied the six balls from
spinner Malcolm Nash for a world-record six successive sixes.
Gary scored runs, took wickets and held catches in majestic
style wherever he played, and he became the best-known and best-
loved cricketer in the world. Barbados came to a halt in 1975
when the Queen visited the sunshine isle of his birth to bestow on
him a well-merited knighthood. Tom Graveney says: 'I played in
the match when Gary made his Test debut and from the moment
he walked on to the field with that animal-like grace of his you
instinctively knew you were in the presence of genius. He was
quite simply, The Greatest.'

JOE SOLOMON
Born: August 26, 1930.
Test record: 27 Tests, 1,326 runs (average: 34.00)
1 century, 4 wickets (average: 67), 13 catches.

Joe Solomon will always have his name linked with the dramatic tied Test in Melbourne in 1960-61. It was his dead-eye throwing that caused two late run-outs and set up the incredible finale. This slender East Indian experimented as an opening partner to Conrad Hunte, but was at his most effective when played in the middle-order where his careful right-handed batting contained bowling attacks while his more illustrious partners plundered runs in quick fashion at the opposite end. He seemed to thrive on tension and drama and he played a key part in the incredible drawn second Test at Lord's in 1963 with an invaluable contribution of 56. His finest Test performances came in India on the 1958-59 tour, during which he made his bow in international cricket. He averaged 117 for the series and scored his one and only Test century when 100 not out in the fifth Test at Delhi. He averaged 41.54 in his 13-year career, and took 51 wickets as a medium-pace leg-break bowler who was sometimes erratic but a regular breaker of stubborn partnerships.

DERYCK MURRAY
Born: May 20, 1943.
Test record: 62 Tests, 1,993 runs (average: 22.90)
181 catches, 8 stumpings.

Deryck Murray was just out of college when Frank Worrell thrust him into the 1963 Test team as first-choice wicket keeper. He belied his boyish looks by performing like a veteran, and he finished the series with a West Indian record of 22 catches and two stumpings. Following his Test baptism, he had two years at Cambridge University with whom he was a successful cricketer but not a model student because his studies took a back seat to his sport. It was not until he moved to Nottingham University while registered with Notts that he got a degree in business studies. He later put his knowledge of law and economy to good use by helping to form the West Indies Players' Association. Deryck came from a family steeped in cricket. His father was a leg-spinner with Trinidad and later a respected administrator, while his uncle was secretary of the famous Queen's Park Club in Port of Spain where Deryck learnt his skills behind the stumps and as a batsman who was sound enough to open for the West Indies during the search to find a partner for Conrad Hunte. He was the first West Indian wicket keeper to claim 100 victims.

WES HALL

Born: September 12, 1937.
Test record: 48 Tests, 818 runs (average: 15.73)
192 wickets (average: 26.38), 11 catches.

Wes Hall still has many supporters as having been the greatest of all West Indian fast bowlers, although most votes would probably go to Mike Holding whose rhythmic style is like watching an action replay of Hall's classical deliveries. Batsmen almost needed binoculars to see Wes start his run-up and when he finally delivered the ball it was always with lightning speed and often lethal bounce. Wes was at his most menacing when he had his partner Charlie Griffith operating at the opposite end. He was the lightning to Charlie's thunder and together they could drive batsmen towards nervous disorders. Standing 6 feet 2 inches and loose muscled, he had the ideal build for a fast bowler and unlimited stamina as he proved when bowling throughout the day in the dramatic drawn Test at Lord's in 1963. His express deliveries were nearly always bang on the right line and length and he could make the ball rise sharply on even the most docile pitches. He had started out as a wicket keeper/batsman, but his switch to fast bowling lifted him into a class of his own. While a tiger with the ball in his hand, Wes was a cheerful and sporting competitor who was never slow to applaud a decent shot by an opponent. It was his warm personality that helped him win a seat as a senator in the Barbados Parliament at the end of his marvellous cricketing career.

CHARLIE GRIFFITH

Born: December 14, 1938.
Test record: 28 Tests, 530 runs (average: 16.56)
94 wickets (average: 28.54), 16 catches.

Charlie Griffith was an exceptionally quick fast bowler, whose career was dogged by controversy. He collected the unwelcome tag of 'Big Bad Charlie' because of his morose, bad-tempered moods when continually picked on by players and press for allegedly throwing his faster ball. Nobody was ever able to prove whether or not his action was illegal, but he was called for throwing in two first-class matches and was always at the centre of debate as to whether his bouncer was chucked rather than bowled. There was never any malice in his partner Wes Hall, but that did not always seem the case with Charlie who frightened the life out of batsmen with his intimidatory tactics. He was at his best – or worst – on the 1963 tour of England when he headed the bowling averages with 119 wickets (12.83), including 32 wickets in the five Tests. There has never been a more feared bowler.

LANCE GIBBS

Born: September 29, 1934.
Test record: 488 runs (average: 6.97)
309 wickets (average: 29.09), 52 catches.

A cousin of Clive Lloyd, Lance Gibbs was a cricketing thorough-bred who for several years held the world record for most wickets in Test matches. His 309 wickets were collected with stylish off-break bowling that featured extraordinary spin and bounce. He developed his essentially English style of bowling in the Lancashire and Durham Leagues before joining Warwickshire with whom he was a popular and successful county bowler. During the memorable 1960-61 series in Australia, he took three wickets with four balls in the third Test and then performed the hat-trick in the fourth Test to underline the fact that he was ready to take over as No. 1 spinner from Ramadhin and Valentine. His most startling Test performance came against India in Barbados in 1961-62 when he claimed 8 second innings wickets for just 6 runs in a spell of 15.3 overs that included 14 maidens.

THEY ALSO SERVED

WILLIE RODRIGUEZ

Born: June 25, 1934.
Test record: 5 Tests, 96 runs (average: 13.71)
7 wickets (average: 53.42), 3 catches.

A damaged knee prevented him making a real impact on the 1963 tour of England. He made his only Test appearance in the fifth and final Test when used as an experimental opener, putting on a useful stand of 78 with Conrad Hunte in the second innings. Rodriguez was a respected all-rounder at home in Trinidad where he scored many useful runs as a reliable right-handed batsman and bowled leg-breaks with accuracy and enthusiasm.

EASTON McMORRIS

Born: April 4, 1935.
Test record: 13 Tests, 564 runs (average: 26.85)
1 century, 5 catches.

Easton McMorris was one of the procession of openers called up by West Indies in their long hunt for a regular partner for Conrad Hunte. He was an efficient right-handed batsman who could gather runs at a fast pace once he had played himself in, but too often – particularly in English conditions – he was unable to handle the early swing of a new ball. He had his greatest success against India in 1961-62 when he averaged a very healthy 58.16.

THE TOM GRAVENEY ASSESSMENT

Frank Worrell's West Indians played England off the park. You only have to look at the averages for the 1963 series to realize that England were outbatted and outbowled. For the first time in a Test series this century not one English batsman reached three figures, and Freddie Trueman was the only bowler who matched their standards with the ball. What baffles me, even 25 years on, is how the selectors could have discarded Brian Statham after only one Test. He was a proven force and would have given Trueman the support he so badly needed in the later Tests by which time several of our batsmen were looking shell-shocked.

Four West Indians – Hunte, Kanhai, Butcher and Sobers – had batting averages of over 40. Only that gritty Yorkshireman Phil Sharpe managed that for England, and he was not selected for the first two Tests. But for Sharpe and some blindly brave batting by Brian Close England would have folded in much more depressing fashion. I was itching for a recall that summer because I really fancied having a go at Hall and Griffith, but the selectors in their wisdom decided I was not the man for the job. Three years later against virtually the same West Indian attack I managed to average 76.50 when creaking on towards my 40th birthday! This is not sour grapes. It's just that I know that the technique of some of our batsmen against the pace of Hall and Griffith was all wrong and they were sitting ducks because of the way they played.

Having said that, I doubt if we could have conquered West Indies if all our batsmen and bowlers had been at the top of their form. Frank Worrell had brought his team to the absolute peak of their power at just the right time, and they revitalized cricket in this country with their dashing style and adventurous attitude. They were a beautifully balanced side. Hall and Griffith have rarely been bettered as pace partners, and Lance Gibbs was an off-spinner of top English class. Then there was that one-man cricket team Gary Sobers able to give support in any bowling style that was required.

They lacked a regular pair of openers, but it rarely noticed because of the consistency of Conrad Hunte. Then there were batsmen of the quality of Kanhai, Butcher and, of course, the multi-talented Sobers. I thought they might have problems with their wicket keeping, but Deryck Murray emerged as a youngster of immense promise who showed he had a magnificent pair of hands when clutching the thunderbolts from Hall and Griffith.

Bringing it all together like a master conductor was skipper

Worrell, who may not have had the playing ability of old but was worth his place in the team on his captaincy alone. He was the man who set the pace and the standards, motivating his players with quiet words of encouragement, and not only preaching but also practising a gospel of attacking cricket.

The West Indians brightened what was a wet and dreary summer with their dynamic cricket and brought pleasure to millions with an approach and attitude that was at one and the same time controlled yet carefree.

Worrell's Wonders will loom large in my thoughts when I come to the final chapter in which I have to decide which was the greatest of all the Test teams. It's going to take a very special combination to beat the 1963 West Indians.

Ali Bacher's
South Africa, 1970

THE SQUAD:

Barry Richards (4)   Lee Irvine (4)   Grahame Chevalier (1)
Trevor Goddard (3)   Mike Procter (4)   Herbert Lance (3)
Ali Bacher (4)   Dennis Gamsy (2)   John Traicos (3)
Graeme Pollock (4)   Peter Pollock (4)   Denis Lindsay (2)
Eddie Barlow (4)   Kelly Seymour (1)   Pat Trimborn (1)

SCOREBOARD: 4 Tests, 4 victories

Figures in brackets indicate the number of Test match appearances

---

BACKGROUND

Ali Bacher's 1969-70 South Africans forced their way into our
Top Ten shortlist because of the impressive fashion in which they
swept aside the challenge of an exceptionally strong Australian
side led by Bill Lawry. It was both an exhilarating yet sad occasion for South African cricket. Just as they proved they had a team
capable of conquering the world, the poison of politics seeped
into the sports scene and the South African cricketers were
pushed into isolation. This was their finest and also their final
hour in official Test competition.

The main strength of the Springboks lay in their powerful
batting line-up. Since their 1967 triumph over Bobby Simpson's
Australians Barry Richards had emerged as potentially the greatest
batsman in the world, and he added his phenomenal talent to that
of established craftsmen like Graeme Pollock, Eddie Barlow, Lee
Irvine, Denis Lindsay and the veteran Trevor Goddard. Mike
Procter had come through as an all-rounder in the Goddard mould
and his pace with the new ball provided an ideal balance to the
accuracy of Peter Pollock. With so many gifted players to call
on, skipper Ali Bacher needed only to do well with the toss to

give them every chance of winning in his first series as captain. Bacher produced what he described as a 'lucky' coin for the toss and won in each of the four Tests. For the man who away from cricket was a doctor in a multi-racial Johannesburg hospital, it was just what the doctor ordered.

TOM GRAVENEY: 'In all the years that Australia have been playing Test cricket I doubt if they have taken such a tanking as they got in South Africa. They were not just beaten. They were annihilated. The smallest total they had to chase in any of the four Tests in the final innings was 452. When Norman Giller and I were putting together our final Top Ten list we had a Bill Lawry team pencilled in, but they had to give way to the Bacher side that would I am sure have dominated world cricket for much of the 1970s if it had not been for the political situation that closed the door to them on the international stage. In Barry Richards they had discovered a batsman who stands comparison with the greatest of all time. Had it not been for his at times casual approach to the game, he would have got the vote of many cricket observers as the undisputed king. When you added the talent of Richards to the grace of the Pollock brothers, the pace of Mike Procter, the power of Eddie Barlow and the experience of Trevor Goddard you had as good a combination as there has ever been in modern cricket. They lacked only an established spin bowler in the class, say, of Hughie Tayfield. That apart it was impossible to find a weak link in their side. Bill Lawry's team certainly didn't find it...'

THE OPPOSITION

Bill Lawry, one of the most reliable opening batsmen of all time, led an Australian team to South Africa that was full of confidence after successful tours of England, the West Indies and India. They were packed with vastly experienced and exceptionally talented players. Along with Lawry there were prolific run-makers of the calibre of Ian Chappell, Doug Walters, Ian Redpath and Keith Stackpole, along with the highly touted Paul Sheehan who had scored an excellent century in India two months earlier. Graham McKenzie was their main strike bowler, and he had support from the big-hearted Alan Connolly. They were rich in the spin department with the off-spin of Ashley Mallett and the mystifying skills of Johnnie Gleeson, an unorthodox spinner who had been baffling some of the finest batsmen in the world. With a squad like that it was understandable that the Australians fully expected to get revenge for the 3-1 series defeat of Bobby

Simpson's tourists in South Africa in 1966-67. What the Aussies clearly didn't realize is that in the three years since they had staged a Test series the South Africans had uncovered a wealth of batting and bowling talent. The Australians also did not take into account the fact that so many of their star players could hit poor form at the same time. Bill Lawry was rarely among the runs in the Test matches following a run-feast start to the tour, and his vice-captain Ian Chappell managed only 92 runs in eight innings. Ian Redpath and Doug Walters were also below their best, and to make matters worse their No. 1 bowler Graham 'Garth' McKenzie lost his way completely and took only one wicket throughout the series. Just to underline their misery, the Australians dropped catches in all the Tests during which their fielding was nowhere near up to their usual high standards.

THE TEST MATCHES
FIRST TEST: Cape Town (January 22-27)

Australia had never been beaten in six previous Tests at the beautiful Newlands ground, but they were always struggling to keep pace with the South Africans in this match from the moment Ali Bacher won the toss in his first Test as captain. Eddie Barlow laid the foundation to the South African first innings total of 382 with a carefully compiled 127 in six hours at the wicket. The Australians were fuming when an appeal was turned down for a catch behind against Barlow off the first ball of the second day, and from then on there was often bad feeling showing between the two fiercely competive sides. Johnnie Gleeson had claimed 18 wickets in the two matches leading up to the Test and he was the bowler the South Africans feared. But he took some hammer in returning 1 for 91, while Ashley Mallett was more successful but expensive with 5 for 126. Bacher (57) played a splendid captain's innings in support of Barlow. The roar of the crowd echoed round Table Mountain when Peter Pollock dismissed both Bill Lawry and Ian Chappell in the space of four balls with just five runs on the scoreboard. Australia never recovered from this nightmare start and despite a plucky 73 from Doug Walters they were all out for 164. With the ball starting to turn, Bacher decided against enforcing the follow-on. Graeme Pollock followed his 49 in the first innings with a 50 in the second as South Africa pushed their lead up to 451 against some intelligent swing bowling from Connolly (5-47). Only Lawry (83) and Redpath (47 not out) put up real resistance and the South Africans won by the comfortable margin of 170 runs. **RESULT: South Africa (382 and 232) beat Australia (164 and 280) by 170 runs.**

Jim Laker, whose 19 for 90 in the 1956 Old Trafford Test lifted him into the land of cricketing legend. He always gave the ball a real tweak and batsmen could almost hear it hum like a spinning top as it left his fingers.

Tony Lock, one of the most competitive spin bowlers of all time. Laker's partner with Surrey and England, he used to spill over with the sort of aggression more usually associated with hostile pace bowlers.

Garfield Sobers, the batsman, shows his batting power for West Indies against England at Edgbaston in 1973. Alan Knott is the wicket keeper.

Garfield Sobers, the bowler, could deliver the ball at speed and with swing or spin. In 93 Tests, he took 235 wickets for West Indies and scored 8032 runs.

Charlie Griffith's suspect bowling action was often under close scrutiny during his 28-Test career with the West Indies in the 1960s.

Rohan Kanhai, a wonderfully gifted batsman who was a permanent fixture in the West Indies side from 1957 to 1974. During the 1960-61 series in Australia, he became the first West Indian to score two centuries in the same Test match. He was a globetrotting runmaker for Guyana, Western Australia and Tasmania as well as becoming a key member of the Warwickshire side. He briefly succeeded Garfield Sobers as West Indies captain.

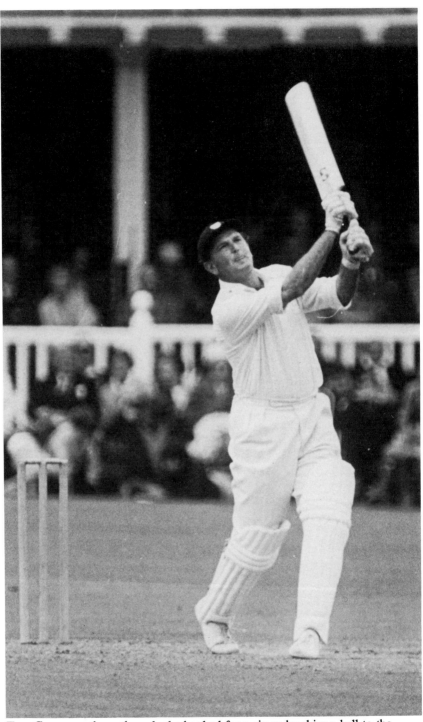
Tom Graveney, the author, looks booked for a six as he skies a ball to the boundary for Worcestershire in his final season as county captain in 1970.

Colin Cowdrey plays firmly off the front foot for Kent with the sort of style
that brought him 22 centuries during a record 114 Tests for England.

Above: Doug Walters, an Australian idol who was rarely able to produce his best form on the playing fields of England, comes down the wicket to attack the bowling of Ray Illingworth at Headingley in 1968.

Left: Richie Benaud was a gifted leg spinner, an aggressive batsman, a tactical genius and one of the most astute and successful Australian captains of all time. He is now the 'Voice of Cricket' on television.

SECOND TEST: Durban (February 5-9)

The open animosity between the two teams was exposed even before a ball was bowled in the second Test. Bill Lawry lodged an official protest after Ali Bacher had ordered an extra cut of the wicket following the toss. The South African skipper, who won the toss and elected to bat, insisted that it had been agreed beforehand that the wicket would be trimmed once more before the start. The argument did nothing to break the concentration of South Africa's brightest young stars. Graeme Pollock and Barry Richards both unveiled the batting form that has won them lasting fame despite their brief exposure on the Test scene. The rampant Richards (140) was just six runs short of a century before lunch on the first morning and reached his 100 off only 116 balls. Then Pollock took over the stage and totally dominated the Australian attack as he piled up 274 runs, including a record sixth wicket partnership of 200 with Hebert 'Tiger' Lance (61). Pollock thrashed 43 boundaries and ran a five during an onslaught that lasted 417 minutes and enabled South Africa to declare at a mammoth 622 for 9. The Australians, demoralized by a succession of dropped catches, never looked like making a fight of it in their first innings reply of 157. Paul Sheahan (62) was top scorer against a combined attack in which Eddie Barlow (3-24) was the most successful. Australia showed more determination when they followed on, but they were left with too high a mountain to climb. Keith Stackpole (71), Doug Walters (74) and Ian Redpath (74 not out) helped push the total up to 336 but it was not enough to stop South Africa scoring an innings victory and going two up in the series with a day to spare. **RESULT: South Africa (622) beat Australia (157 and 336) by an innings and 129 runs.**

THIRD TEST: Johannesburg (February 19-24)

The punishment continued for Australia at the New Wanderers ground. They went into the match without the unwell Graham McKenzie, and literally tossed away the chance of getting into the game by dropping another procession of catches after South Africa had again won the toss. Barry Richards (65) and Graeme Pollock (52) led the run charge as they had in Cape Town, and Lee Irvine (79) weighed in with a valuable knock that pushed the first innings total up to 279. Australia made a disastrous start against the pace of Peter Pollock (5-39) and Mike Procter (3-48) and slumped to 12 for 3, with Lawry, Stackpole and Redpath all back in the pavilion. Chappell (34), Walters (64) and Sheahan (44) staged a recovery until another collapse from 190 for 6 to

202 all out. The feature of South Africa's second innings was a another enterprising century by Eddie Barlow (110), with Graeme Pollock (87) and Lee Irvine (73) giving excellent support on the way to another massive total of 408. Johnnie Gleeson had eight match wickets as consolation for being hammered for 186 runs. Only Redpath (66) and last-man-in Connolly (36) got above 20 runs as the dispirited Australians crashed all out for 178 and to a comprehensive defeat by 307 runs. Connolly fell to a catch by Richards off the bowling of Trevor Goddard, who announced after the match that he was retiring from Test cricket following a frank exchange of views with the selectors. So Goddard took a wicket off his final ball of a Test career that was one of the most distinguished in the history of South African cricket.

FOURTH TEST: Port Elizabeth (March 5-10)

Ali Bacher won the toss for the fourth successive time in the four-Test rubber, and once again he elected to bat. Richards (81) and Barlow (73) shared the first century opening partnership of the series before some inspired bowling by Alan Connolly (6-47) put the brake on and South Africa finished their first innings with a total of 311. Yet again spilt catches cost the Aussies dear. Peter Pollock (3-46) and Mike Procter (3-30) gave the Australian batsmen a torrid time and only Redpath (55) and Sheahan (67) got above 20 in a first innings reply of 212. Richards flourished the full range of his vast repertoire of shots as he raced to 126 in the second innings, passing the 500 run mark for the series on the way and lifting his average for the rubber to 72.57. Ali Bacher also looked to be set for a century until treading on his wicket with his score at 73. It provided the only Test wicket of the series for the strangley subdued Graham McKenzie, whose best-forgotten series analysis was 1 for 333. Australia's fielding calamities continued and their misery was somehow encapsulated in the way Lee Irvine reached his maiden Test century, Redpath dropping a catch at fine leg and watching the ball roll to the fence for a four as a gale-force wind whipped around the ground. Denis Lindsay hit a middle-order 60 in a total of 470 for 8 declared. The Australians, looking as if all they wanted to do was get home as quickly as possible, were given a glimmer of hope when Peter Pollock limped off with a pulled hamstring muscle after just one over. But Mike Procter just bowled with twice as much fire despite a 'flu bug and took 6 for 73 as the Australians tumbled all out for 246, beaten by a record margin of 323 runs. Sheahan (46) and Lawry (43) were their top scorers. **RESULT: South Africa (311 and 470) beat Australia (212 and 246) by 323 runs.**

THE CAPTAIN

Doctor Aron (Ali) Bacher was an amateur cricketer, with a purist's approach to the game. An intellectual, he was a thoughtful tactician much in the mould of England's Mike Brearley. His deep understanding of the game followed his specialized coaching at King Edward's School in Johannesburg where he came under the influence of former Somerset professional H.T.F. (Bertie) Buse. He was an outstanding all-rounder who shone at soccer, Rugby, squash and baseball as well as being a sound right-handed batsman and excellent fielder, often playing behind the stumps with success.

Born on May 24, 1942, he combined his cricket with a distinguished medical career and after getting his degree at Witswatersrand University, he was appointed as a house doctor at the multi-racial hospital in Johannesburg. He played for his province, Transvaal, from the age of 18 and became their respected captain. In 1965 he toured England with South Africa and collected 1,008 runs at an average 40.32. During his career he scored 7,894 runs (39.07), held 110 catches and completed 18 centuries.

His highest score was 235 for Transvaal against Bobby Simpson's Australian tourists at Johannesburg in November 1966. Many onlookers considered his performance in that game one of the greatest match-winning efforts they had ever seen from an individual. His magnificent innings, then a Springbok record against an overseas team, sent the Aussies reeling to their first defeat on South African soil for 64 years. He augmented a personal match aggregate of 280 runs with five brilliant catches, and shared a fourth wicket stand in the second innings of 237 with 'Tiger' Lance. Bacher played several crucial innings for South Africa during his 12 Test matches. He contributed an invaluable 67 to help South Africa to victory over England in the 1965 Trent Bridge Test, and his 60 not out during an undefeated century stand with Graeme Pollock saw the Springboks home to a win against the Australians at Durban in 1966-67.

But it is for his firm, authoratitive captaincy against Lawry's Australians in his one and only series in charge that he is revered in South Africa. He continually out-thought the Aussies, and impressed oberservers with his field placings and the way he kept the pressure on the opposition at the first scent of victory. Throughout a dream of a series that was a nightmare for Australia he did not make one wrong decision. Bacher put his success down to his 'lucky' coin with which he won the toss every time. *Test record:* 12 Tests, 679 runs (average: 32.33),10 catches.

TOM GRAVENEY: 'Ali Bacher's captaincy during the 1969-70 series against Australia was a wonderful example of how positive leadership can inspire and motivate a team. We were all looking forward to seeing how he and his marvellously talented side would fare against England just a couple of months after their triumph over Bill Lawry's team when, at the eleventh hour, the South African tour of England was cancelled for political reasons. Now this is not the place for me to comment on the rights and wrongs of mixing politics with sport, but I know that Dr Bacher shares my loathing for the fact that politicians too often use sport as a platform for their views. We always hear about the bad and the unjust things happening in South Africa, but how much publicity was given to the fact that Dr Bacher came out of retirement to play for a black team in the newly formed Transvaal Mixed Leagues? He has continually argued the cause of bringing South Africa back into the international cricket arena, and with sport not politics as his motivation. Ali was the cricketing hero of the Transvaal and was carried shoulder high off the pitch after playing his final Currie Cup match to concentrate full time on his career as a senior house doctor at a multi-racial hospital in Johannesburg. Now manager of the South African Cricket Union, he continues to build bridges that he hopes will one day see a South African team – picked purely on ability – back on the Test circuit.'

THE PLAYERS

BARRY RICHARDS
Born: July 21, 1945.
Test record: 4 Tests, 508 runs (average: 72.57)
2 centuries, 1 wicket (average: 26), 3 catches.
Barry Richards was a naturally gifted right-handed opening batsman of the very highest class, and it is cricket's tragedy that politics prevented him from having a regular international stage upon which to demonstrate his remarkable batting skills. Because of the pressures on them not to fail, openers are usually defence-minded, cautious characters. Not so Barry Richards who right from the first ball would be looking to let his elegant stroke-play flow. If he did have a weakness it was a lack of total concentration and commitment at all times. Such was his extraordinary depth of talent as a batsman that he would occasionally become disinterested and complacent at the thought of plundering another massive innings. He was at the very start of what would unquestionably have been an illustrious Test career when South Africa were banished from international cricket. His

brief Test experience spanned the four matches against Bill Lawry's Australians, but even in that short time he proved to the world that he was a genius of a batsman. Richards was in demand around the world when not accumulating runs for Natal in the Currie Cup competition. He used to make the South Australia scorer work overtime in Sheffield Shield matches, and on the playing fields of England he shared a long-running partnership at Hampshire with West Indian opener Gordon Greenidge. His most stupendous innings came for South Australia against Western Australia at Perth in 1970-71 when he streaked to 325 runs in a single day on his way to his highest score of 356. He returned to the international arena in the late 1970s following the Kerry Packer revolution and was a successful performer in the World Series Cricket tournament in Australia. Tall and upright, Richards was a classical straight hitter who had perfect technique and excellent timing that enabled him to play the ball later than most batsmen. He was also an inventive off-spin bowler who once took 7 for 63 for Hampshire against the Rest of the World team at Bournemouth in 1968. King Barry retired in 1983 with a mountain of 28,358 first-class runs at an average of 54.74 and 80 centuries to his name. There have been batsmen who have scored more runs, but few have put them on the scoreboard with quite the same style and flair.

TREVOR GODDARD
Born: August 1, 1931.
Test record: 41 Tests, 2,516 runs (average: 34.46)
1 century, 123 wickets (average: 26.22), 48 catches.
Trevor Goddard was a tall and powerfully built all-rounder who was an imposing sight when opening both the batting and the bowling for South Africa. A consistent rather than explosive player, he was a regular and reliable servant for South Africa from the late 1950s until the third match of the final series against Bill Lawry's tourists. He was an authoritative, if limited, left-handed opening batsman who played solidly off the back foot. He scored 18 half-centuries in Test matches, but reached the century mark only once when striking 112 against England in Johannesburg in 1965. He was a lethal left-arm seam bowler who could whip in the occasional faster ball that caught many fine batsmen napping. His accurate line and length and variations of pace and movement kept batsmen and close-wicket fielders on their toes. He was a consistent wicket taker at Test level and took five wickets in an innings five times. His best bowling return in Test cricket was 6-53 against Australia in 1966-67. He is the only South African to have taken 100 wickets and accumulated 2,000

runs in Test cricket, a double that he completed in his 36th Test match. Goddard was also a capable close fielder who held 48 catches for his country. In 1959-60 he scored 200 for Natal against Rhodesia and took 6 for 3, including the hat-trick, against Border at East London. One of his most memorable innings was against Australia at Cape Town in 1957 when he scored 56 not out and carried his bat through an innings of 99. He captained South Africa 13 times, winning once and losing twice. A competitive captain, he was also a sporting one as he showed when recalling Mike Smith in a 1965 Test match at Johannesburg after the England skipper had been 'run out' while going down the pitch to do some 'gardening'. Goddard asked the umpire to reverse the 'out' decision. Winning was important to him, but not everything.

GRAEME POLLOCK
Born: February 27, 1944.
Test record: 23 Tests, 2,256 runs (average: 60.97)
7 centuries, 4 wickets (average: 51), 17 catches.
Graeme Pollock was, along with Neil Harvey and Gary Sobers, possibly the greatest left-handed batsman the game of cricket has seen. He had the poise, the strokes and the temperament to make himself a formidable opponent at all times and in all conditions. As with Barry Richards, it is difficult to measure his standing in international cricket because of the Test ban on South Africa, but there is no doubt that he can be bracketed with the all-time greats. He was just 26 and had scored two centuries against England and five against Australia when the iron curtain dropped on his Test career. He did not follow the globe-trotting example of Richards, and so the great pity is that not too many people outside South Africa had the pleasure of watching him at his peak. Graeme announced his great potential when at the age of just 16 he scored a century for Eastern Province in a Currie Cup match. It was the start of one of the greatest of all batting careers. While he was essentially an attacking batsman, he had a strong defensive foundation and was an absolute master when going back on his back foot to control the shorter pitched ball. His positioning, balance and footwork were superb, and while a tall and powerfully built man he was a 'touch' player, preferring to glide and glance the ball to all parts of the ground. He used the bat like an artist's brush, painting technicolor innings wherever he played. Anybody who was at Trent Bridge in 1965 will know that is no exaggeration. He stroked his way to 125 runs with effortless ease against a battery of England bowlers who were unanimous in praising his performance even though he did grievous harm to

their averages. Pollock made his Test debut in 1963-64 against Australia, and scored 122 in the third Test at Sydney, followed by 175 in the next Test at Adelaide. He went on to score five more Test centuries including two brilliant double centuries – 209 against Australia in 1966-67, and 274 against Australia in 1970. The innings of 209 was memorable for his courage as much as his class. He came to the wicket with a pulled muscle and had to have a runner. South Africa looked deep in trouble at 85 for 5 but Pollock pulled them back into the match with a magnficent display of batting, particularly considering his injury handicap. Forced to play most of his shots off his back foot, he raced to his first hundred off 139 balls and completed his innings in 350 minutes after adding 85 for the ninth wicket, with his brother Peter playing the support role at the opposite end. Captains liked to save his energies for batting, but whenever called on he could cause even the soundest batsmen problems with well-flighted right-arm leg breaks. He retired from cricket in 1986, after a highly successful series for a South African XI against an Australian 'rebel' side. During his glittering career he scored over 20,000 first-class runs and made more than 60 centuries. He and his elder brother Peter rate high among the most talented of all cricketing family double acts.

EDDIE BARLOW
Born: August 12, 1940.
Test record: 30 Tests, 2,516 runs (average: 45.74)
6 centuries, 40 wickets (average: 34.05), 35 catches.
Beefy, bespectacled Eddie Barlow was one of the most powerful all-round cricketers ever to play Test cricket. He was not a pretty sight when batting or bowling but he was full of energy and belligerence and breathed fire and life into every match in which he played. His attitude was never less than positive and his 'let's-up-and-at-'em' mood used to spread to his team-mates. Eddie was a stubborn right-handed opening batsman, who was particularly strong off the back foot and once entrenched at the wicket he was very difficult to dismiss. He compiled six centuries in his 30 Tests before the South African ban, and he could be equally effective with the ball as a right-arm medium-pace bowler. Playing for the Rest of the World against England at Headingley he took 7 for 64 including the hat-trick and four wickets in five balls. He could swing the ball either way but was often erratic with his direction. His highest Test score was made against Australia in 1963-64 when he hammered 201 in the fourth Test at Adelaide. His best bowling in a Test was 5-85 against Australia in 1966-67. A top-class slip fielder with over 300 catches to his credit, he galvan-

ised Derbyshire as a demanding captain during a three-year spell and he hit a career-best 217 against Surrey at Ilkeston. Eddie played in the World Series tournament before retiring to concentrate on his South African pig farm, later returning to England as a business representative.

LEE IRVINE
Born: March 9, 1944.
Test record: 4 Tests, 353 runs (average: 50.42)
1 century, 2 catches.
Lee Irvine was a talented left-handed batsman who liked to attack the bowling right from the start of his innings. He possessed a wide range of strokes all around the wicket and specialized in hitting sixes. His potential was spotted while he was still at school and he played in the same Durban Under-14s side as Barry Richards. He made his Test debut in South Africa's last series against Australia in 1969-70 and was highly successful, scoring two half-centuries in the third Test at Johannesburg, and 102 in the second innings of the fourth Test at Port Elizabeth. He scored most of his 7,245 first-class runs for Natal and Transvaal and had a two-year spell at Essex in 1968 and 1969 when he entertained crowds all over the country with his cavalier and often reckless batting. He was also a fine fielder and a useful wicket keeper.

DENIS LINDSAY
Born: September 4, 1939.
Test record: 19 tests, 1,130 runs (average: 37.66)
3 centuries, 57 catches, 2 stumpings.
Denis Lindsay was a thoroughbred cricketer with an excellent pedigree. His grandfather was a South African Test cricketer in the 1920s and his father, John Lindsay, was a highly respected wicket keeper with North-Eastern Transvaal who played in three Tests on the 1947 Springbok tour of England. He encouraged his son to follow in his footsteps, and he did it in style – playing, like his father, for both North-Eastern Transvaal and South Africa. His wicket keeping was polished and efficient, but it was as a batsman that he really flourished. Denis had to live in the shadow of the great batsman-wicket keeper John Waite for the early part of his career, but managed to win a place in the South African Test team on the strength of his batting alone. He made national headlines during a tour of England in 1961 with the Fezelas. Facing Essex leg break bowler Bill Greensmith in the first tour match at Chelmsford, he played the first ball back to the bowler and then proceeded to crash the next five deliveries over the boundary for five successive sixes. In 19 Test matches he

amassed 1,130 runs (37.66) including three centuries. His highest Test score was 182 against Australia in Johannesburg in 1966-67 when he shared a record seventh wicket stand of 221 with skipper Peter van der Merwe. He then equalled the world Test wicket keeping record of six dismissals in an innings when holding six catches. He clung on to 57 catches in all behind the wicket in Test matches and had two stumpings. His career-highest score was 216 against Transvaal B at Johannesburg in 1966-67 during a season in which he averaged 72.42.

HERBERT LANCE
Born: June 6, 1940.
Test record: 13 Tests, 591 runs (average: 28.14)
12 wickets (average: 39.91)
Nicknamed 'Tiger', Herbert Lance was a competitive player who gave useful support to the front-line players with both the bat and the ball. In 13 Test matches he averaged 28.14 as a middle-order batsman and took 12 wickets at an average 39.91 as a change medium-fast bowler. He was a more prolific runmaker in Currie Cup matches and averaged 34.87 over a 13-year career from 1958. Playing for Transvaal against Eastern Province in 1966-67, he scored a century in both innings and his second 100 was beefed up with 10 sixes and 7 fours. The previous season he shared in a record tenth wicket partnership of 174 for Transvaal against Natal. He is best remembered in England for his performance in the third Test at The Oval in 1965 when he contributed 69 in the first innings and then 53 in the second during a bright fifth wicket stand of 96 with the talented Colin Bland. His highest Test score was 70 as South Africa piled up 620 runs against Australia at Johannesburg in 1966-67.

MIKE PROCTER
Born: September 15, 1946.
Test record: 7 Tests, 226 runs (average: 25.11)
41 wickets (average: 15.02), 4 catches.
There have been few more dynamic all-rounders than Mike Procter, and he along with Graeme Pollock and Barry Richards was a truly world-class player robbed of international fame by South Africa's isolation because of their political policies. He won the affection and admiration of English cricket followers during a 16-year career with Glouccstershire, a county he captained from 1977 and to whom he gave sterling service both with the bat and the ball before a recurring knee injury forced his retirement in 1981. He hit 1,000 runs in an English season nine times and took 100 wickets in a season twice. His highest knock in England was

203 for Gloucestershire against Essex in 1978. He equalled a world record in 1970-71 when he completed a century in each of six successive innings for Rhodesia. In the same season he compiled the highest score of his first-class career with 254 for Rhodesia against Western Province. His batting alone would have guaranteed him a place in any team in the world; and the same can be said of his bowling. He had a bulldozing run-up and he would release the ball with lightning pace, seeming to be on the wrong foot at the moment of delivery but never at the expense of accuracy. To complete his all-round ability, he could also bowl slow off-spin on a turning pitch and the standard of his fielding matched all the other departments of his game. His best bowling return was 9 for 71 for Rhodesia against Transvaal at Bulawayo in 1972-73. It was his always lively and at times hostile fast bowling that wrecked the Australians in the 1969-70 series when he finished with 26 wickets at 13.57. His bowling style may have been unorthodox but it was certainly effective, as a procession of Australian batsmen would be prepared to testify.

PETER POLLOCK
Born: June 30, 1941.
Test record: 28 Tests, 607 runs (average: 21.67)
116 wickets (average: 24.18), 9 catches.
The sons of a journalist who edited the *Eastern Province Herald* after playing for Orange Free State, Peter and Graeme Pollock were the favourite sons of South African cricket. There was no question that Graeme was the more talented player, but Peter – three years older – was in no way overshadowed and would rank high on any rating list of post-war fast bowlers. He headed both the Test and first-class bowling averages when South Africa toured England in 1965 (Graeme topped the batting averages). Peter's most successful tour was in 1963-64 when he claimed 40 wickets in eight Tests in Australia and New Zealand. He and Mike Procter were a formidable double act with the new ball and between them took 41 of the 80 Australian wickets that fell during South Africa's triumphant final Test series in 1969-70. Standing nearly 6 feet 3 inches tall, the strongly built Pollock made a noteable start to his Test career when in his debut against New Zealand at Durban in 1961-62 he finished with match figures of 9 for 99. His most memorable tour match was at Trent Bridge in 1965 when his 5 for 53 and 5 for 34 helped South Africa win the Test against England. It was a match that belonged to the Pollocks. Graeme scored a magnificent 125 in the same Test. Peter could prove a stubborn or adventurous tail-end batsman as the situation dictated.

ATHANASIOS TRAICOS
Born: May 17, 1947.
Test record: 3 Tests, 8 runs (average: 4.00)
4 wickets (average: 51.75), 4 catches.
Eygptian-born Athanasios (John) Traicos was a lower-order right-handed batsman and a right-arm off-break bowler who had his only Test experience in the 1969-70 series against Australia. He was studying at Natal University when called into the squad and he played in three of the four Tests, but without making a real impact. He toured England in 1967 with South African Universities and in his first-class debut against Cambridge University at Fenners he took 5 for 54 in the first innings. He toured England again in 1982 with Zimbabwe. The best bowling return of his career was 6-66.

THEY ALSO SERVED

PAT TRIMBORN
Born: May 18, 1940.
Test record: 4 Tests, 13 runs (average: 6.50)
11 wickets (average: 23.36), 7 catches.
He took more than 300 wickets for Natal with lively right-arm fast bowling that earned him four Test caps, his first one coming at the relatively late age of 26. In 1969 he toured England with the International Cavaliers and played a full season in the Lancashire League with East Lancs, claiming 91 wickets at an inexpensive 7.89 and topping 500 runs. His bowling in the second innings (3-12 off 10 overs) played a major part in South Africa's victory over Bobby Simpson's Australians in the 1966-67 Port Elizabeth Test when the Springboks clinched victory in the rubber.

DENNIS GAMSY
Born: February 17, 1940.
Test record: 2 Tests, 39 runs (average: 19.50)
5 catches.
One of the few bespectacled wicket keepers, Dennis Gamsy rivalled Denis Lindsay for the position of South Africa's No. 1 keeper following the retirement of John Waite. He was not quite in Lindsay's class with the bat but was still a useful performer, often opening the batting for Natal. He had a fast pair of hands and stumped 33 batsmen during his career and held on to 277 catches. He made an eventful debut for Natal in the Currie Cup in 1959-60 when he dismissed nine batsmen during the match. His career-best score with the bat was 137.

MICHAEL SEYMOUR
Born: June 5, 1936.
Test record: 7 Tests, 84 runs (average: 12.00)
9 wickets (average: 65.33), 2 catches.
Michael (Kelly) Seymour was, like Ali Bacher, a practising doctor who combined a cricket career with his medical work. He was a right-arm off-break bowler who announced his arrival as a class spinner when taking 12 for 152 for South African Universities against the New Zealand tourists at Pretoria in 1961-62. He was never able to show his domestic form in the Test arena and the nine wickets he took in his seven Test match appearances were extremely expensive. He broke a finger when failing to take a catch from Ian Redpath off the bowling of Barry Richards in the first Test against Bill Lawry's Australians and took no further part in the series.

GRAHAME CHEVALIER
Born: March 9, 1937.
Test record: 1 Test, 5 wickets (average: 20.00)
1 catch.
A left-arm slow bowler with Western Province, Grahame Chevalier claimed the valuable wicket of Paul Sheahan (caught Eddie Barlow) in his first over in Test cricket. It was one of five wickets he took in the first Test of the 1969-70 series for 100 runs, his one and only appearance on the international stage.

THE TOM GRAVENEY ASSESSMENT

I was a player-coach with Queensland at the time that the Australians returned from their nightmare 1969-70 tour, and I knew from the shell-shocked reaction of their players that they had come up against an extraordinary force in South Africa. Excuses, some of them legitimate, were made for their dismal showing. They *were* tired following a tour of India immediately before the South African series. They *were* handicapped by the complete loss of form of their main strike bowler Graham McKenzie. They *were* unlucky to lose the toss in every match. And they *were* unfortunate to have several debatable umpiring decisions going against them. But having accepted all that there were no excuses that could explain away one of the most crushing defeats in the history of Test cricket. There could be only one conclusion: the Australians had been outplayed by an immensely gifted team.

I'm not usually one for dropping statistics into an argument – I prefer flesh and blood facts. But the figures of that 1969-70 Test series tell their own story of South Africa's overwhelming superiority. The Springboks scored six centuries and built five century partnerships to none by Australia. They averaged 40 runs per wicket throughout the series to just 22 by Bill Lawry's team. Ian Chappell had a miserable time with just 92 runs in 8 innings, and poor Graham McKenzie could show only one wicket for 333 runs that were conceded in just three matches.

We had known before the tour started that the two Pollock brothers—Graeme in particular—along with Trevor Goddard and Eddie Barlow were top-flight performers. But it was the emergence of Barry Richards and Mike Procter as phenomenally gifted players that turned South Africa from being a very good side to, yes, a great one.

The tragedy is that because of the poison of politics we were never able to see them at their peak. But in that one astonishing series they achieved enough to carry a lot of weight in our argument as to which has been the greatest of the post-war Test teams.

Ian Chappell's Australia,1974-75

THE SQUAD:

Ian Redpath (6)	Doug Walters 6)	Jeff Thomson (5)
Wally Edwards (3)	Rodney Marsh (6)	Ashley Mallett (5)
Ian Chappell (6)	Terry Jenner (2)	Rick McCosker (3)
Greg Chappell (6)	Dennis Lillee (6)	Geoff Dymock (1)
Ross Edwards (5)	Max Walker (6)	

SCOREBOARD: 6 Tests, 4 wins, 1 defeat, 1 draw

Figures in brackets indicate the number of Test match appearances

BACKGROUND

The England team that set off for Australia late in 1974 bounced with confidence after three series without defeat under the leadership of Scotsman Mike Denness. Four months later on the way home they were a shell-shocked squad, still reeling from the twin tornado that had ripped through them and blown their composure and self-assurance to pieces.

Australia were well and truly back as a power in the game, and it was to remain that way while they were able to call on the sensational pace partnership of Dennis Lillee and Jeff Thomson. Lillee made nonsense of the fact that he had been been written off as finished following three stress fractures of the lower spine. Even at a slower, more controlled pace England's batsmen still found him too fierce and fast to handle. But their biggest shock came from the relatively unknown Thomson, who before the 1974-75 series had played in just one Test match against Pakistan two years earlier when he returned 0-100 and 0-10. He came at the England batsmen like a rocket-engined bat out of hell and they just had no answer to his sheer blinding speed.

It was Ian Chappell who had started to pump the pride back into Australian cricket following their humiliation in South Africa and then a slump at home against an England team led by Ray Illingworth and inspired by John Snow. Chappell took over the reins from Bill Lawry and his demands for a more committed and competitive approach met with immediate success with a shared series in England and victories over Pakistan, West Indies and New Zealand. He had the brilliant talent of his younger brother Greg, the opening patience of Ian Redpath and the drive of Doug Walters to bolster the batting, plus the superlative wicket keeping of Rodney Marsh and useful support bowling from big Max Walker. But most of all he had found a partner for Dennis Lillee.

TOM GRAVENEY: 'Australia had at last discovered a pace combination fit to be mentioned in the same breath as that great pair Lindwall and Miller. The arrival of Thommo as a fearsome force eased the pressure on Lillee, who had been shouldering too much responsibility. With Thomson holding a one-man blitz at the opposite end Dennis was able to concentrate more on line and length, and he became an even more effective bowler as he varied his pace and direction. I rated him much the better craftsman of the two but in that 1974-75 series it is doubtful if any but a handful of bowlers have approached the stunning speed generated by Thomson. A year later he had his speed of delivery scientifically measured at 99.6 mph. Lillee was timed at 86.4 mph. Those two outstanding West Indian pace men Andy Roberts and Michael Holding were timed at 93.6 mph and 92.3 mph respectively. So Thommo was close to being a ton-up man. Whatever speed he was bowling at it certainly proved too fast for most of the England batsmen. Another important asset was the emergence of Rodney Marsh as a reliable keeper after a dodgy start to his career when he collected the nickname "Iron Gloves". His keeping, particularly off the bowling of Lillee, was as vital to Australia as that of Godfrey Evans had been in his days standing up to Alec Bedser. Rodney had a simple pact with Dennis: "You bowl 'em, I'll catch 'em." Lillee and Marsh together became as effective a tandem team as Lillee and Thomson.'

THE OPPOSITION

A lot of controversy clouded England's original team selection. Geoff Boycott was picked, but then decided he did not wish to tour. It was an open secret that he was not the greatest admirer of skipper Mike Denness. Brian Luckhurst was Boycott's replacement in a squad from which John Snow – magnificent on the last tour to Australia – was strangely omitted. The pace bowling was in the hands of Bob Willis, Peter Lever, Geoff Arnold, Chris

Old and Mike Hendrick, with Fred Titmus and Derek Underwood providing the spin. All-rounder Tony Greig was available with medium-pace or spin, as conditions demanded. John Edrich, Dennis Amiss, Keith Fletcher, David Lloyd and Greig joined Denness as batsmen with a lot of potential runs between them, and Alan Knott travelled as first-choice wicket keeper with Bob Taylor as his deputy. England were handicapped by injuries throughout the tour and at one time front-line bowlers Bob Willis, Mike Hendrick and Peter Lever were out of action. There was an even bigger crisis among the batsmen when both Edrich and Amiss had hands put in plaster after taking knocks from fast balls in the first Test. This led to an emergency call for 41-year-old Colin Cowdrey to make a return to the Test scene after more than three years out of international competition; and to add to all his woes Denness could hardly get his bat to the ball after fighting off a mystery virus at the start of the tour. He eventually became the first captain in Test history to drop himself. All in all it was not the happiest of England squads.

THE TEST MATCHES

FIRST TEST: Brisbane (November 29-December 4)

Skipper Ian Chappell (90) and his brother Greg (58) were top scorers in an Australian first innings total of 309 accumulated on an unreliable pitch that had been hastily prepared following a storm that had swept the ground. Another storm was waiting to hit England in the shape of Jeff Thomson. Tony Greig (110) held the first innings together with a bold and fearless century, the first for England at Brisbane since Maurice Leyland hit 126 back in 1936-37. It lifted England's reply to 265 against some, to put it mildly, lively bowling from Thomson (3-59), Lillee (2-73) and Max Walker (4-73). A quick dart for runs by Greg Chappell (71), Ross Edwards (53), Doug Walters (62 not out) and Rodney Marsh (46 not out) enabled Ian Chappell to declare at 288 for 5. England started the final day at 10 for 0, but then got their first real taste of Thomson in full flight and were rushed out for 166. Thommo took 6 for 46 and perhaps more important from Australia's point of view he had sewn seeds of doubt in the minds of several England players about their ability to cope with him. Derek Underwood was top scorer with a brave 30. England's only cause for celebration was that Alan Knott overhauled the Test record of 173 catches held by his predecessor with England and Kent, Godfrey Evans. **RESULT: Australia (309 and 288) beat England (265 and 166) by 166 runs.**

SECOND TEST: Perth (December 13-17)

Within four days of arriving in Australia as an emergency batsman, Colin Cowdrey found himself out in the middle facing the full fury of Lillee and Thomson after three years off the Test stage. England were put into bat and totalled 208, with Cowdrey contributing 22 before being bowled by Thomson. Knott (51) and Lloyd (49) were top scorers. Ross Edwards (115), Doug Walters (103) and Greg Chappell (62) hammered the England bowlers as Australia replied with a colossal 481. Walters zipped to his century between tea and the close of play on the second day, reaching his 100 with an audacious six off the last ball of the session bowled by Bob Willis. Thomson (5-93) ripped the heart out of the England second innings. Freddie Titmus, playing his first Test match for seven years at 42, was top scorer with 61 in a total of 293. Australia held on to 17 of the 18 chances that went to hand and Greg Chappell set a new Test record for a non-wicket keeper by pouching seven catches. Australia got the winning runs for the loss of one wicket on the fourth day. **RESULT: Australia (481 and 23-1) beat England (208 and 293) by nine wickets.**

THIRD TEST: Melbourne (December 26-31)

Ian Chappell again won the toss and invited England to bat before a Boxing Day crowd of 77,165. Lillee (2-70) and Thomson (4-72) put the England batsmen under a lot of pressure and none of the recognized batsmen really got settled. Alan Knott (52) was top scorer in a total of 242. Mike Hendrik pulled a muscle in his third over and it was left to Willis to give a spirited bowling performance and he was rewarded with a return of 5-61 that kept the Australian reply down to 241 despite a firm foundation innings by opener Ian Redpath (51). England opener Dennis Amiss was caught for 90 – a frustrating two runs short of Bobby Simpson's record aggregate of 1,381 runs in a calendar year (since passed by Vivian Richards). Tony Greig (60) and David Lloyd (44) helped push the second innings total up to a respectable 244. Thomson (4-71) took eight wickets in the match. Needing 246 runs to win, Australia started the final day at 4 for 0. Greg Chappell (61) seemed to have put Australia in sight of victory but they lost their way and with an hour of play left still required 55 runs with four wickets in hand. An inspired spell by Greig (4-56) and some deadly accurate bowling from Titmus and Underwood tied the tail-end down and the Aussies were still eight runs short with two wickets standing when time ran out. **RESULT: Match drawn. England (242 and 244), Australia (241 and 238 for 8).**

FOURTH TEST: Sydney (January 4-9)

Australia regained the Ashes four years after losing them to Ray Illingworth's team on the same ground. Out-of-form skipper Mike Denness dropped himself and John Edrich took over as captain. John has painful memories of the game because as well as a defeat he also suffered two cracked ribs from one of Lillee's express deliveries. Australia were put on the way to an emphatic victory by a first innings total of 405, with Greg Chappell (84), debutant Rick McCosker (80) and Ian Chappell (53) making valuable contributions against determined bowling by Geoff Arnold (5-86) and Tony Greig (4-104). Edrich (50) and Alan Knott (82) were the only batsmen to dig in against another wave of effective bowling from Lillee (2-66), Thomson (4-74) and Max Walker (2-77) as England laboured to a reply of 295. A superb second wicket stand of 220 betwen Ian Redpath (105) and Greg Chappell (144) meant Australia were able to declare at 289 for 4. A thunderstorm washed out the last sesssion of the fourth day and on the final day Ashley Mallett (4-21) produced some enterprising off-spin after Lillee (2-65), Thomson (2-74) and Walker (2-46) had caused the usual consternation among England's batsmen. Greig battled to 54 with little support. **RESULT: Australia (405 and 289 for 4 dec.) beat England (295 and 228) by 171 runs.**

FIFTH TEST: Adelaide (January 25-30)

After the first day was washed out, Mike Denness put Australia into bat in conditions tailor made for the left-arm spin of Derek Underwood who took 7 for 113. But savage knocks by Terry Jenner (74), Doug Walters (55) and Max Walker (41) boosted the Australian total to 304. Denness (51) and Keith Fletcher (40) were the exceptions in a pathetic reply of 174 by England, with the pace of Lillee (4-49) and Thomson (3-58) once again proving their downfall. It brought Thomson's haul in the series to 33 wickets, and – much to England's relief – it was to be his last act of plunder because after damaging a shoulder playing tennis on the rest day he was sidelined for the rest of the season. A knee injury restricted Bob Willis to just five overs in Australia's second innings and Walters (71 not out), Rodney Marsh (55), Ian Redpath (52) and Ian Chappell (41) all helped themselves to runs that enabled a declaration at 272 for 5. Underwood finished with match figures of 11 for 215. Gallant Alan Knott scored only the second century by a wicket keeper in the history of the Ashes but his 106 not out and a painstaking 63 by Keith Fletcher could not save England. **RESULT: Australia (304 and 272 for 5 dec.) beat England (172 and 241) by 163 runs.**

SIXTH TEST: Melbourne (February 8-13)

Peter Lever, Mike Denness and Keith Fletcher were the heroes as England salvaged some self-respect from a nightmare series. But their decisive victory in this sixth and final Test was robbed of a lot of gloss by the fact that Thomson was missing and Lillee bowled only six overs before retiring injured. Lever gave the Australians some of their own medicine on the first day, taking 6 for 38 on a damp wicket as they tumbled for a total of 152 of which Ian Chappell scored a fighting 65. Denness at last excelled with the bat, showing enormous character as he battled his way to 188 which remains the highest score by any England captain in Australia. After having made only one century stand in the previous five Tests, England now enjoyed three in succession: 149 by Edrich (70) and Denness for the third wicket, 192 by Denness and Fletcher (146) for the fourth wicket, and 148 by Fletcher and Tony Greig (89) for the fifth. England finally amassed 529 in the face of some wholehearted swing bowling by Max Walker (8-143). Having siezed the initiative for the first time in the series, England were determined not to let it go and despite stiff resistance from Greg Chappell (102), Ian Redpath (83), Rick McCosker (76) and Ian Chappell (50) they forced a long-awaited victory by an innings and four runs. **RESULT: England (529) beat Australia (152 and 373) by an innings and 4 runs.**

THE CAPTAIN

Ian Chappell combined a fierce competitive spirit with a general's command of cricket strategy to become one of Australia's greatest captains. He was a demanding skipper who insisted on total endeavour from his players, and he always set an example with personal commitment that was never less than 100 per cent. The leading part he played in helping to set up the revolutionary Kerry Packer World Series circus diminished him in the eyes of the cricket Establishment, but nothing anybody says can hide the fact that he had outstanding ability as a cricketer and as a captain. If anything, he was *too* eaten up by a win-at-all-costs attitude that meant that good sportsmanship often took a back seat when Australian teams under his influence were scenting victory.

Ian comes from a family rich in cricket history. His grandfather, Victor Richardson, captained South Australia and Australia in the 1930s, and he inherited his tactical brain. His two brothers, the enormously gifted Greg and youngest brother Trevor, have been Test players and all of them were being taught the art of cricket almost as soon as they could walk, and each of them received specialized coaching at Adelaide's Prince Alfred College.

Ian made his debut for South Australia at the age of 18 and within three years was in the Test team, selected mainly for his aggressive right-handed batting but also for his genius as a slip fielder, and less so for his useful leg-break bowling. He had that vital big match temperament and was always able to produce the performance that most suited the needs of his team. His highest score in Test cricket was 196, and he almost matched it with 192 in his final Test as captain against England at The Oval in 1975 before handing over the reins to his brother Greg. It's with Greg that he holds a uniqe batting record. They became the first and only brothers to each score a century in both innings of the same Test match – against New Zealand in Wellington in 1973-74. Ian scored 145 and 121, Greg a career-best 247 not out and 133.

But it was as a captain that Ian made his biggest mark on international cricket. The Australian game was in the doldrums following depressing defeats by South Africa and Ray Illing-worth's England when Ian was named as successor to Bill Lawry. He sent a hurricane of change blowing through the Test team and moulded and motivated the Australians into a side worthy of comparison with their great predecessors. The first two matches under his banner were lost but by a side that had not been sufficiently influenced by him. Once he had been given the time to get his ideas and theories across there was not an Australian Test player who would not have walked barefoot across the pitch on hot coals had he asked it of them.

He was, of course, fortunate to have Dennis Lillee and then Jeff Thomson at the peak of their powers under his leadership, but it was his great tactical knowledge that brought the best out of them. They always bowled to fields that were perfectly set and were used in exactly the right spells of a match to maximize their effect. *Test record:* 75 Tests, 5,345runs (average: 42.42), 14 centuries, 105 catches, 32 wickets (43.71). Captain in 30 Tests (won 15, lost 5, drew 10).

TOM GRAVENEY: 'There have been few shrewder captains than Ian Chappell, who knew how to squeeze the last drop out of any situation that might help give his team an advantage. He was an absolute master at putting pressure on the opposition with just the right run rate or with a field that could be almost impossible to pierce. Yes, he was fortunate to have Lillee and Thomson in his firing line, but it was his captaincy that inspired them to give that little extra that made all the difference. Some of his tactics were quite intimidatory and stank of out-and-out gamesmanship that

116

made old pros like me wince. It was an open secret that he used to encourage his players to give a lot of verbal abuse to rival batsmen when they were at the wicket in an attempt to break their concentration. You may be appalled by that, but Ian was a tough Aussie who considered all fair in love, war and cricket. You didn't find him whingeing if anybody gave him stick back. It just made him that more determined to win. Like it or not, that's the modern game. While not in the same class as his brother Greg as a batsman – only a handful of players in history can probably claim to have been that – Ian was a very accomplished player, and Bobby Simpson is the only Australian I've seen with a safer pair of hands at slip. His deep involvement in the "Kerry Packer Affair" should not be allowed to cloud the fact that he was an exceptional cricketer and a very successful captain for Australia.'

THE PLAYERS

IAN REDPATH
Born: May 11, 1941.
Test record: 66 Tests, 4,737 runs (average: 43.45)
8 centuries, 83 catches.
By the end of the 1974-75 series the England players were not only scared of the sight of Lillee and Thomson but sick of the sight of opening batsman Ian Redpath. He batted for a total of 32 hours during the six Tests, and continually gave the Australians a firm foundation on which to build their run mountains. A patient rather than prolific scorer of runs, he frustrated a procession of fast bowlers for more than a decade on the Test scene after replacing Bobby Simpson as Bill Lawry's regular opening partner. He was a loyal servant to Victoria throughout his 14-year career, stepping into the shoes of the highly respected Colin McDonald in 1962. 'Redders' was a tall, lean technically sound batsman who collected his runs quietly and without fuss, leaving the hurricane hitting to partners better equipped for the job of scoring at a fast rate of knots. There have been few finer players of quick bowlers, and even when the ball was coming through at head height from the fastest of the West Indian bowlers he was able to play the ball with what seemed like time to spare. He averaged 52.27 against the West Indies in 1975-76 when the likes of Roberts, Holding and Keith Boyce were firing on all cylinders. His highest score in Test cricket was 171 when batting at No. 5 against Ray Illingworth's England at Perth in 1970-71. He was an eagle-eyed close fielder who held 83 Test catches. A charming

and popular man who took an active interest in politics, Redpath made a brief comeback with World Series Cricket that ended when he injured himself leaping in delight to celebrate a rare wicket as a bowler.

RICK McCOSKER
Born: December 11, 1946.
Test record: 25 Tests, 1,622 runs (average: 39.56)
4 centuries, 21 catches.
Rick McCosker announced his arrival as a batsman of considerable talent when in his debut for Australia in the fourth Test against England in the 1974-75 series he shared an opening stand of 96 with Ian Redpath and finished with a confidently struck 80. A bank worker in Sydney, he desposited many fine innings during his tour of England in 1975 and averaged a remarkable 82.80 for the four Test matches. He will always have painful memories of the Centenary Test at Melbourne in 1977. He mistimed a hook against England fast bowler Bob Willis and the ball broke his jaw. He showed his courage and character by returning to the crease with his jaw wired to score valuable runs that helped Australia win the match. His highest Test score was 127 against England at The Oval in 1975. The England bowlers led by his bogeyman Willis exposed his weakness outside the off-stump on a less productive tour with Australia in 1977.

GREG CHAPPELL
Born: August 7, 1948.
Test record: 87 Tests, 7,110 runs (average: 53.86)
24 centuries, 47 wickets (average: 40.70), 122 catches.
A classical front-foot player, Greg Chappell always looked quite majestic at the wicket and imperiously in control of all that was happening around him. His elder brother Ian was more functional and essentially a back-foot player. If you could have got a balanced mixture of the two, you would have had the *perfect* batsman. As it was there were many who considered that Greg fitted that bill with his upright stance, high back lift and powerful follow-through. He was elegant and stylish in everything he did and his range of shots covered just about every stroke in the book. His driving, particularly on the on-side, was never bettered by any batsman. While essentially an attacking player, he had a sound defence that enabled him to dig in if ever match circumstances called for a more cautious approach. In the true Chappell tradition, he was a magnificent slip fielder as his record 122 Test catches prove, and he could also turn his hand to tight and tidy medium-pace bowling. He spent a short but successful time playing County cricket with Somerset in the late 1960s when the

experience of playing on English wickets served him well in later seasons. His captaincy when taking over from brother Ian was less demonstrative, but his leadership was by example as he showed in his first match as skipper when compiling 123 and 109 against the 1975-76 West Indies side that the following summer took Tony Greig's England apart. Greg scored 702 runs in all during that first series as captain for an astonishing average of 117. Australia have had a long production line of marvellous batsmen. Greg Chappell ranks with the very best of them, and he would have plenty of supporters who would argue that he was *the* greatest of them all.

ROSS EDWARDS
Born: December 1, 1942.
Test record: 20 Tests, 1,171 runs (average: 40.37)
2 centuries, 7 catches.

Ross Edwards, a sound rather than spectacular right-handed middle-order batsman, found out what an unpredictable game cricket can be in the space of three weeks on his first tour of England in 1972. Playing in his second Test at Trent Bridge he came in as an emergency opener in the second innings and scored an impressive 170 not out. Then in the third Test at Headingley later the same month he was humbled by the batsman's nightmare of a pair. Edwards had followed his father into the Western Australian side as a batsman-wicket keeper, but with Rodney Marsh entrenched in the Test team he became a specialist batsman whose safe hands proved invaluable in the covers where he was famed and feared for his swooping catches. He averaged 50.60 in the 1975 Test series in England following a couple of outstanding knocks in the Prudential World Cup. An accountant by profession, he played World Series Cricket before moving to New South Wales in 1979.

DOUG WALTERS
Born: December 21, 1945.
Test record: 74 Tests, 5,357 runs (average: 48.26)
15 centuries, 49 wickets (average: 29.08), 43 catches.
One of the great mysteries of cricket is that Doug Walters – one of the great post-war heroes of Australian cricket – failed to score a single century in four tours of England. Wherever else he played Walters was an undisputed master of the batting arts, but he rarely looked comfortable against seam bowling on unpredictable English wickets. He was a born entertainer who used to look to get his wide array of strokes flowing from the moment he took

119

guard, and so he was handicapped on any wicket that did no offer true bounce. English bowlers found him a far different proposition on his home pitches and in his first Test series against England in 1965-66 he scored centuries in two of his opening three innings. He was at his most prolific against the West Indies in the 1968-69 series at home when he stroked his way to 699 runs in four Tests. His haul included 242 and 103 at Sydney in the fifth Test, the first time a batsman had ever scored a double century and a century in the same Test. He also became the first post-war Australian to score six fifties in consecutive innings and the first to score four hundreds in a rubber against West Indies. And this was against the might of Hall, Griffith and Sobers. He punished the West Indian bowlers on their own territory in 1973 when he averaged 71.00 for the series and included in his output a startling century between lunch and tea at Port of Spain. In 1976-77 he put together his highest Test score – 250 against New Zealand at Christchurch. A small, bouncy character, he always had a special rapport with the Australian public and was the darling of the spectators at Sydney where he played dozens of dashing innings for New South Wales.

RODNEY MARSH
Born: November 11, 1947.
Test record: 96 Tests, 3,633 runs (average: 26.51)
3 centuries, 343 catches, 12 stumpings.
Rodney Marsh was a combative, belligerent wicket keeper whose winning-is-all approach to each game captured the competitive spirit that Ian Chappell implanted in the Australian team. In his early appearances as first-choice wicket keeper he struggled to maintain the high standards of his predecessors. But having shrugged off the unkind nickname of 'Iron Gloves' he developed into a safe and often spectacular keeper whose handling against the lightning-quick deliveries from Lillee and Thomson was a vital factor in Australia's run of success in the 1970s. The line 'caught Marsh, bowled Lillee' appeared a record 95 times in Test scorebooks. He and Lillee were also a formidable double act together in Sheffield Shield matches for Western Australia. The brother of outstanding golfer Graham Marsh, he gradually won the affection and admiration of English cricket followers who at first mistook his aggressive attitude for bad sportsmanship. But Rodney was for all his toughness a fair-minded cricketer who simply refused to admit defeat until the final ball of a match had been bowled. There have been few more formidable wicket keeper-batsmen, although he lacked the necessary consistency to command a place high in the batting order. Beefily built, he used

to get full power into lusty left-handed straight drives and could scatter a field with a volley of boundary shots. He could also when necessary present the straight, orthodox defensive bat. Rodney scored the first ever Test hundred by a specialist Australian wicket keeper and he turned the Centenary Test of 1977 in Melbourne into a show stage for himself by scoring 110 not out and overtaking his schoolboy hero Wally Grout's Australian record of 187 dismissals. He set a world record for most dismissals by a wicket keeper in Tests with 343 catches and 12 stumpings.

MAX WALKER
Born: September 12, 1948.
Test record: 34 Tests, 586 runs (average: 19.53)
138 wickets (average: 27.47), 12 catches.

Big Max Walker – 6 foot 4 inches tall and built to last – came to Melbourne from his native Tasmania with the idea of concentrating on a full-time career in Australian Rules Football. But like those talented Tasmanians before him, Jack Badcock and Ted McDonald, he made his main impact in the cricket world. Max seemed to do everything wrong as a medium-pace bowler, delivering the ball off the wrong foot after running in with an ungainly whirling windmill action that suggested he might trip over his own feet. This was why he was nicknamed 'Tangles'. But for all his lack of coaching-book orthodoxy, he was an effective bowler as his 138 wickets in Test matches proved beyond argument. He could hit an accurate line and length and was able to swing the ball into the bat or cut it away off the wicket. Max came from a cricket-mad family and he is full of stories about his early days in Tasmania where he and his father were the stars of the local village team. He tells the improbable tale of how he and his father once won a match by running 17 off the last ball after Walker senior had appeared to send the ball hurtling into long grass, with every member of the opposition going off to search for it. If that doesn't stretch the imagination to breaking point, Max has an even more unblieveable punchline to the story. He swears that his father was batting with a length of paling ripped off the pavilion fence after one of their team's only two bats had been mislaid. After they had crossed for their 17th and winning run his father held up the makeshift bat to show the ball impaled on a six-inch nail! A tall story from a tall man who lit up cricket grounds wherever he played with his swinging bowling and enthusiastic batting. He had unlimited stamina and was as strong as a bull, as he proved with his 8 for 143 figures in the final 1974-75 Test.

DENNIS LILLEE

Born: July 18, 1949.
Test record: 70 Tests, 905 runs (average: 13.71)
355 wickets (average: 23.92), 23 catches.

Dennis 'The Menace' Lillee had two great careers as a fast bowler on the way to building a reputation as one of the most deadly wicket takers in the history of cricket. Lillee Mark 1 was a terrorizingly quick and aggressive new ball bowler who could devastate teams with the sheer pace of his deliveries. He first burst on to the Test scene in the sixth and final Test of the 1970-71 series against Ray Illingworth's England in Adelaide. He took 5 for 84 in partnership with a pace man called Thomson – not Jeff, but Alan. A year later he firmly established himself as a world-class strike bowler when in five Tests in England he claimed what was then an Australian overseas record of 31 wickets (17.67). His career at the top seemed over when stress fractures in his back temporarily forced him out of the game. Then Lillee Mark 11 fought his way into the Australian firing line and, while lacking his early fearsome speed, he was even more deadly because of his uncanny accuracy and his ability to move the ball either way. He was associated with two winning partnerships, operating at his best when Rodney Marsh was keeping wicket, and having his most effective support when Jeff Thomson was bowling at the opposite end. He would sometimes allow his competitive spirit to spill over into bad temper, but he never lost the respect of the public and colleagues and opponents alike for ability and character that made him one of the most accomplished bowlers of all time. Lillee was the first bowler to take 350 Test wickets and held the world record for most wickets until overtaken by Ian Botham who is on record as calling Dennis 'the perfect bowler'.

ASHLEY MALLETT

Born: July 13, 1945.
Test record: 38 Tests, 430 runs (average: 11.62)
132 wickets (average: 29.84), 30 catches.

Ashley Mallett is considered by many good judges to have been the finest Australian off-spin bowler of the last 40 years. He first made an impact when collecting 111 wickets during a season with Ayr in the Scottish Western Union. After taking 32 wickets in his first eight matches with South Australia he was called up for the 1968 tour of England but played only in the final Test at The Oval and finished with match figures of 5 for 109. A sharp spinner of the ball and always accurate with his line and length, he earned a recall to the Test arena after taking 13 for 122 in a Shield match against Western Australia. He was happiest operating on pitches

122

where he could get bounce as well as spin, and he had his most successful series in India in 1969-70 when he finished with 28 wickets including 10 for 144 at Madras. His best one-innings performance came against Pakistan at Adelaide in 1972-73 when he claimed 8 for 59 off 23.6 overs. He was a brilliant fielder, particularly in the gully and held 30 catches in Test cricket. As a tail-end batsman, he could be stubborn when keeping his wicket intact was all important and he once showed scoring as well as staying ability when putting together an innings of 92 for South Australia against Western Australia in a 1971 Sheffield Shield match. His highest score in Test cricket was 43 not out against England at the Oval in 1968 when making his debut.

JEFF THOMSON
Born: August 16, 1950.
Test record: 51 Tests, 641 runs (average: 12.09)
200 wickets (average: 27.03), 19 catches.
Many people thought Jeff Thomson was just making excuses for his dismal performance when he claimed after his sterile Test debut that he had kept secret the fact that he was bowling with a broken bone in his foot. His figures of 0-100 and 0-10 against Pakistan in 1973 seemed to point more to a broken heart. It was 1974-75 before the selectors almost reluctantly gave him a second chance against Mike Denness's England team. The rest is history and as he knocked England wickets and batsmen over the majority view suddenly swung to the opinion that he must have been telling the truth about that foot injury. The impact he made in that series will never be forgotten, particularly by the England batsmen who were on the receiving end of some of the most ferocious bowling since the 'bodyline' tour 40 years earlier when it had been the Aussies dodging the thunderbolts from Larwood and Voce. A rebel without a pause off—and sometimes on—the pitch, 'Thommo the Terror' collected world-wide headlines at work and play with his anti-Establishment behaviour, and in his early days was happier surf riding than chasing round cricket grounds. But when giving the game his full attention and when free of his considerable injury problems he was one of the fastest and most feared bowlers ever to step foot on a cricket pitch. He lacked the accuracy of his plundering partner Dennis Lillee and was often erratic with his deliveries, but he had no equal for being able to make a ball lift and kick and put batsmen in fear of their lives. He collected 200 Test wickets and might have had many more but for a recurring shoulder injury which first gave him serious problems when he damaged it playing tennis on the rest day of the fifth Test of the 1974-75 series.

THEY ALSO SERVED

WALLY EDWARDS
Born: December 23, 1949.
Test record: 3 Tests, 68 runs (average: 11.33).
Wally Edwards was a forceful left-handed opening batsman who was discarded by the Australian selectors after managing only 68 runs in three Tests during the 1974-75 series against England. He lost his place to Rick McCosker after being trapped lbw for a duck by Tony Greig in the third Test of the series. His top score was 30 in a stand of 64 with Ian Redpath in the first innings of the second Test, but he got a duck in the second innings.

GEOFF DYMOCK
Born: July 21, 1946.
Test record: 21 Tests, 236 runs (average: 9.44)
78 wickets (average: 27.12), 1 catch.
Geoff Dymock was a medium-fast left-arm strike bowler who created a unique record against India in Kanpur in 1979-80 when, in returning match figures of 12 for 166, he became the first Australian to dimiss all 11 batsmen during the two innings in a Test. He produced another excellent solo show with a match analysis of 9 for 86 in helping Australia beat Mike Brearley's England by 138 runs in the first Test of their mini series in 1979-80. A favourite with Queensland, he could make the new ball dip and swerve when conditions suited him but was often used more as a stock bowler than a strike bowler at Test level. He had a disappointing trip to England in 1977 when he took only 15 wickets against County sides and was unable to win a Test place against the competition of Jeff Thomson, Max Walker and Len Pascoe. He was recalled when the Kerry Packer revolution decimated the Australian team.

TERRY JENNER
Born: September 8, 1944.
Test record: 9 Tests, 208 runs (average: 23.11)
24 wickets (average: 31.20), 5 catches.
A right-arm leg-break bowler, Terry Jenner bowled in tandem with Ashley Mallett for South Australia but was unable to clinch a regular place in the Test team. His most impressive bowling performance was against West Indies in Port of Spain in 1972-73 when he took 5 for 90 in the first innings, including the key wickets of Roy Fredericks, Alvin Kallicharrran, Rohan Kanhai and Keith Boyce. His highest Test score as a tail-end batsman was 74 against England in the fifth Test of the 1974-75 series.

THE TOM GRAVENEY ASSESSMENT

It came as a severe shock to the nervous system of the England batsmen when Australia suddenly produced the twin terrors Lillee and Thomson. Nobody had seen such fast and hostile bowling 'down under' since the 1954-55 series when Frank 'Typhoon' Tyson was hurling them down for England against Ian Johnson's Australians. I deliberately toss Tyson's name into this assessment because during that tour he produced the quickest bowling I have ever seen. I was fielding in the slips and we were having to stand 40 yards off the bat, and *still* the ball was often going over our heads off edged shots. The bowling of Thomson in particular reminded me of Tyson at his fastest and deadliest, and my heart went out to the England batsmen. I think the technique of several of the England batsmen left a lot to be desired, but all the coaching and textbook reading in the world could not have prepared them for the sort of short-pitched deliveries that kicked head high and at something approaching 100 mph.

The pace of Thomson and the deadly accuracy and cunning of Lillee unnerved England and I honestly don't believe that Mike Denness had sufficient stature and experience as a player and captain to help his batsmen get over what were deep psychological wounds, particularly as he himself was having such a wretched time of it with the bat. If you are not confident on a cricket field you are in trouble and Lillee and Thomson crushed England's confidence early in a tour that turned into a nightmare. It is significant that Tony Greig and Alan Knott—going in at six and seven—were the most consistent run gatherers for England. There might have been a different story to tell had their team-mates matched their teeth-gritting fighting qualities.

With Lillee and Thomson in his gunbelt, Ian Chappell was like a quick-on-the-draw sharp-shooter and he was not the type of captain to show a moment's mercy once he got the victory taste. The Australian batting was always solid and often sparkling, and Rodney Marsh was a marvel behind the stumps. But it was those two terrors of pace Lillee and Thomson who guarantee this Australian team having a considerable presence in the final chapter when I have to choose the *greatest* of the great teams.

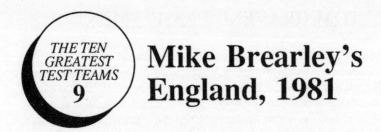

THE TEN GREATEST TEST TEAMS 9

Mike Brearley's England, 1981

THE SQUAD:

Geoff Boycott (6)	Bob Taylor (3)	Chris Old (2)
Graham Gooch (5)	John Emburey (4)	Mike Hendrik (2)
David Gower (5)	Graham Dilley (3)	Wayne Larkins (1)
Mike Brearley (4)	Bob Willis (5)	Paul Downton (1)
Mike Gatting (6)	Bob Woolmer (2)	Paul Parker (1)
Peter Willey (4)	Chris Tavare (2)	Paul Allott (1)
Ian Botham (6)	Alan Knott (2)	

SCOREBOARD: 6 Tests, 3 wins, 1 defeat, 2 draws

Figures in brackets indicate the number of Test match appearances

---

BACKGROUND

Mike Brearley led England teams to victory in 18 out of 31 Tests and lost only four times, a record of consistency and success that stands comparison with that of the greatest captains in the history of English cricket. We have selected the team that retained the Ashes against the Australians in 1981 to represent him in this *Greatest Test Teams* argument even though he took over as captain only after the first two matches had been played. It gives us the opportunity to spotlight possibly the most incredible Test series ever staged, and to bring into the debate the quite stunning solo performances of one of the most charismatic, yet at the same time controversial characters of the modern game: Ian Terence Botham.

When the 1981 series started, Botham was England captain. He took over the leadership when Brearley stepped down in the summer of 1980 after helping to build a team—both in stature and in spirit—that was a match for the best in the world. Botham's captaincy did not work the same magic and England went 12 matches without a win. After the drawn second Test against

Australia in 1981 he resigned, a decision that saved the selectors from what was looming as an inevitable sacking. The Aussies were 1-0 up in the series and it was the old sage Mike Brearley whom the selectors invited to try to save the Ashes.

TOM GRAVENEY: 'I thought the selectors were wrong to give the captaincy to Ian Botham in the first place. He is an out-and-out individualist who thrives on going about things in his own unconventional way, and with a swagger and a gambler's instinct that is hardly suitable to team leadership. There is no question that he is an exceptionally gifted cricketer, probably the greatest English all-rounder of all time. To captain England in Test cricket you must have great strength of character, self-discipline, an understanding of man-management, a total grasp of cricket tactics and the ability to mould and motivate a collection of individuals into a team. In the recalled Mike Brearley England had just the man for the job. Brearley's reappointment as captain left Ian free from the shackles of responsibility and he proceeded to flourish matchwinning skill of a kind never before seen on an English cricket ground. They were performances he would not have been able to produce as captain because he would have been anchored by convention and the restraining knowledge that he should not take chances.'

THE OPPOSITION

There was a blow to Australia before a ball was bowled. Greg Chappell announced that he needed a rest from cricket, so the Aussies lost their captain and No. 1 batsman. Kim Hughes was the man selected to take his place, a gentleman of the game and a batsman nearly in the Chappell class but not nearly so competitive. Their main strike bowler Dennis Lillee was rarely 100 per cent fit throughout the tour and both Rodney Hogg and Geoff Lawson were hit by injury. But they did have an extraordinary find in Terry Alderman, a swing bowler who found English conditions suited him down to the ground. Rodney Marsh was now the most experienced and successful wicket keeper in the world, taking over from Alan Knott during the tour as the leading catcher in Test cricket. In Ray Bright, Australia had a left-arm spinner who could make things difficult for even the greatest batsmen on any pitch that offered him encouragement. And, above all else, Australia had Allan Border who chose this tour to establish himself as a batsman who could be mentioned in the same breath as other great left-handers like Neil Harvey, Graeme Pollock, Gary Sobers and Clive Lloyd. What Australia *didn't* have was an all-rounder in the class of I.T. Botham.

THE TEST MATCHES
FIRST TEST: Trent Bridge (June 18-21)

This was the first Test match in England to include Sunday play, and Australia produced their Sunday best to win on the Sabbath when Trevor Chappell – the third of the brothers to play for his country – made the winning hit in his Test debut. It was the old war horse Dennis Lillee who pushed England to the edge of defeat with a match analysis of 8 for 80, and his new plundering partner Terry Alderman gave the sort of support that sent shivers down the spines of English batsmen with match figures in his Test debut of 9 for 130. In a low-scoring game during which the ball was always beating the bat, only Mike Gatting and Allan Border dug in for reasonable knocks. Gatting scored 52 in England's first innings total of 185 and Border, dropped when 10, struck 63 in Australia's reply of 179. Bob Woolmer collected a 'pair' in his comeback match as England struggled against the swing of Alderman and Lillee, who was slower than at his peak but just as difficult to master because of cunning changes of direction and pace. When Rodney Marsh caught Woolmer in the second innings it took him past Alan Knott's world record of 244 Test dismissals. Skipper Botham (33) was top scorer in an abysmal England second innings total of 125. Graham Dilley (4-24) gave Australia early shocks but they reached their victory target for the loss of six wickets. A major difference between the two teams was that Australia held their catches in magnificent style while England spilled six chances. **RESULT: Australia (179 and 132 for 6) beat England (185 and 125) by four wickets.**

SECOND TEST: Lord's (July 2-7)

Kim Hughes won the toss and put England in for the second successive Test. He must have wondered if he had done the right thing when Graham Gooch cut loose with a swift 44, but his partner Geoff Boycott – playing his 100th Test – was in his tortoise mood and took 100 minutes scoring 17 before becoming one of Geoff Lawson's seven first innings victims for a return of 81. Mike Gatting (59) and Peter Willey (82) pushed the England score along but the last six wickets fell for 27 in a total of 311. Allan Border (64) was again top scorer for Australia in a reply of 345 of which 55 were extras. Boycott spent 240 minutes compiling 60 in a second innings in which David Gower (89) boosted the total to 265. Botham, in what was to be his last match as skipper, collected an embarrassing 'pair'. Graeme Wood (62 not out) held the Australian second innings together and a frustra-

Mike Procter, the dynamic South African and Gloucestershire all-rounder, whose Test career embraced just seven matches between 1967 and 1970.

Barry Richards, an opening batsman with an extraordinary depth of talent, shows his batting flair with Hampshire in a 1972 county match against Lancashire. Farokh Engineer is the wicket keeper.

Graeme Pollock, who used to glide and glance the ball to all parts of the field, gives Hampshire a taste of his talent during South Africa's tour of England in 1965. Bryan Timms is behind the stumps.

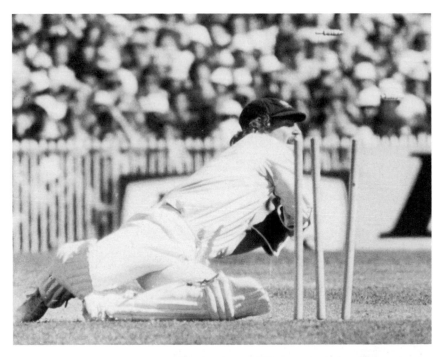

Rodney Marsh, who was once known as 'Iron Gloves' but developed into a safe and often spectacular wicket keeper. He set a world record for most Test dismissals by a wicket keeper between 1970 and 1983 with 343 catches and 12 stumpings in 96 Test matches. He was one of the great appealers of cricket, as Pakistan's Javed Miandad (right) can testify after being trapped lbw by Bruce Yardley in the third Test against Australia at Melbourne in 1982.

Ian Chappell, an aggressive competitor for Australia with the bat and as a
captain, powers the ball away during the 1965 Lord's Test against England.

Greg Chappell, a genius of a batsman for Australia, straight drives for four on his way to 117 runs against England at Perth in 1982.

Dennis Lillee shows the style that brought him 355 Test wickets for Australia as he runs in for an express delivery against England at Trent Bridge in 1972.

Jeff Thomson, one of the fastest and most feared of all bowlers when at his peak, took 200 wickets in 51 Tests for Australia between 1972 and 1982.

ting match played in poor light conditions petered out to a draw. **RESULT: Match drawn. England 311 and 265, Australia 345 and 90 for 4.**

THIRD TEST: Headingley (July 16-21)

Australia looked to have built an unassailable lead when they declared at 401 for 9, with John Dyson (109), Kim Hughes (89) and Graham Yallop (58) leading the run race in the face of some determined bowling from Botham (6-95). Recalled skipper Mike Brearley was invited to bat again after England had crashed all out for 174 of which Botham contributed an aggressive 50. Late on the fourth day at 135 for 7 in their second innings England had just distant hopes of avoiding an innings defeat. Many of the England players had already checked out of their hotel. Then Botham, supported by an inspired Graham Dilley, turned the match – and the series – on its head with an heroic and quite astonishing innings. He smashed a century off only 87 balls as he and Dilley (56) put on 117 in 80 minutes for the seventh wicket. Botham (149 not out) then put on 67 with Chris Old and Australia from looking certain winners suddenly found themselves wanting 130 runs to win the match. Botham's batting had electrified the England team in general and Bob Willis in particular. He produced the bowling display of his life and took a career-best 8 for 43 as Australia's last nine wickets tumbled for 55. England won by 18 runs to become the first team this century to win a Test match after following-on. **RESULT: England (174 and 356) beat Australia (401 for 9 dec. and 111) by 18 runs.**

FOURTH TEST: Edgbaston (July 30-August 2)

Miracle Man Botham transformed this Test with the ball just as emphatically as he had with the bat at Headingley. England looked doomed to defeat after totalling 189 and 219 against the swing of Alderman (match figures: 8-107) and the spin of Ray Bright (match figures: 7-88). In a match in which no batsman reached 50, Australia scored 258 in their first innings and needed just 142 to win with nine second innings wickets standing when Botham struck. He was reluctant to bowl at first on a pitch on which off-spinner John Emburey was worrying the Aussies, but he was persuaded by Mike Brearley that it was the right time and place for his swing. Australia looked to be coasting to victory at 96 for 3, and then sensationally lost their last six wickets for 16 runs in 47 minutes. Botham thrilled a capacity Sunday crowd by taking 5 wickets for just 1 run off 28 balls. **RESULT: England (189 and 219) beat Australia (258 and 121) by 29 runs.**

FIFTH TEST: Old Trafford (August 13-16)

This game has been described by all those who saw it and many who just heard about it as the greatest Test match ever played; and, of course, that man Botham was at centre stage with the innings of a lifetime that had him being mentioned in the same breath as cricketing legends Grace and Jessop. England batted first and scraped 231 against spirited bowling by Dennis Lillee (4-55), Terry Alderman (4-88) and debutant Mike Whitney (2-50), who was brought into the team because of injuries. A tortoise and hare innings from Chris Tavare (69) and Paul Allott (52 not out) saved England from a rout. Botham got a duck. Australia's first innings occupied just 30.2 overs and they were hurried out for 130 after Bob Willis (4-55) had dismissed John Dyson, Kim Hughes and Graham Yallop in his third over. Martin Kent (52) was the only batting success and when he was caught behind he became recalled Alan Knott's record 100th Australian Test victim. England appeared to have thrown the iniative away on the fourth day when they collapsed to 104 for 5. Then Botham arrived at the wicket and hammered his way into the land of cricketing legend. While the immoveable Tavare at the opposite end was completing the slowest 50 in English first-class cricket (306 minutes), Botham opened those wide shoulders of his and proceeded to knock Lillee and Alderman all over the ground. He included five huge sixes in galloping to a century off just 86 balls, and made it an Ashes record of six sixes before being caught by Rodney Marsh off the bowling of Whitney for 118. Tavare's 78 took a little over seven hours yet in its own way was just as important for England, as were the tail-end blasts from Knott (59) and Emburey (57). Shell-shocked Australia tried to save the match and the Ashes with gritty batting by left handers Graham Yallop (114) and Allan Border (123 not out), who was handicapped by a fractured finger. But despite the brilliance of Border, they were all out 103 runs short of their target. This was the Test in which Geoff Boycott overtook Colin Cowdrey's record aggregate of 7,624 runs, but it will for always be remembered simply as 'Botham's Match'. **RESULT: England (231 and 404) beat Australia (130 and 402) by 103 runs.**

SIXTH TEST: The Oval (August 27 to September 1)

This first sixth Test of a series in England became a statistician's delight: a debut hundred for Australia by Dirk Welham; Geoff Boycott's 21st Test and 124th first-class hundred; Dennis Lillee's best-ever match figures of 11 for 159; Terry Alderman's record

42 wickets in a series; Allan Border's second undefeated hundred in successive innings; Botham's 10 match wickets despite carrying an injury and including his 200th Test wicket in record time; Brearley's 50th Test catch and a record 19th unbeaten home Test in his farewell match as England captain. But for all the plethora of facts and figures the one thing the match did not provide was a positive result. It ended in an honourable draw in what just had to be an anti-climax after all that had gone before. The highlight of the match was the duel between old rivals Boycott and Lillee. Boycott (137) came out on top in the first innings before Lillee (7-89) had him caught by Yallop, but Dennis had the last word by trapping Boycott for a duck in the second innings when defiant batting by Gatting (56), Brearley (51) and, in particular, Alan Knott (70 not out) prevented the Aussies from salvaging a victory as consolation for the damage done to them by man-of-the-series Botham. **RESULT: Match drawn. Australia (352 and 344 for 9 dec.), England (314 and 261 for 7).**

THE CAPTAIN

Mike Brearley is respected throughout the world of cricket as having been one of the most perceptive and intelligent tacticians in the modern game. A successful Middlesex skipper from 1971, he succeeded Tony Greig as leader of England in 1977 and was never a loser in 19 Tests at home. His only four defeats in 31 matches as captain were all in Australia.

Born in Harrow in 1942, Brearley was a batsman-wicket keeper in his early career and developed into an outstanding slip fielder capable of snapping up the half chance. In four years as a Cambridge University blue from 1961 he amassed what remains a university record haul of 4,348 runs. A steady rather than spectacular accumulator of runs, he completed 1,000 runs in a season 11 times and topped the 2,000 mark in 1964. His highest score in first-class cricket was an unbeaten 312 for MCC against North Zone at Peshawar in 1966-67. The nearest he came to a Test century was 91 against India in Bombay in 1977 before taking on leadership responsibilities. Despite giving a good deal of his concentration to cricket while at university he still managed to get a first in Classics, which is a pointer to the intellectual depth he brought to his captaincy. *Test record:* 39 Tests, 1,442 runs (average 22.88), 52 catches. Captain in 31 Tests (18 wins, 4 defeats, 9 draws).

TOM GRAVENEY: 'Had he been judged on his batting alone, Mike Brearley would have been remembered as just another pretty good batsman. I have never been one for believing that a captain should win an automatic place in a team. He should earn it with his ability and so win the respect of his players. Mike Brearley was the exception. He fully justified his England place by his command as a captain. His biggest strength was more as a psychologist than as a player. He knew how to get the most out of each individual by saying the right thing at the right time, particularly in the case of Ian Botham who seemed to be twice the player under Brearley's influence. His knowledge of cricket tactics was second to none and his field placings were always spot-on and designed to put the maximum pressure on the opposition with the minimum risk of conceding runs. His record as England captain speaks for itself, and it would have been fascinating to see how he would have handled an England team against the West Indies which was a series that never came under his umbrella. Aussie fast bowler Rodney Hogg summed up Brearley best of all when he was introduced to him for the first time and said, "I've heard about you – you're the man with the degree in people." That was Mike Brearley – a master at man-management and cricket captaincy, and a pretty good bat.'

THE PLAYERS

GEOFF BOYCOTT
Born: October 21, 1940.
Test record: 108 Tests, 8,114 runs (average: 47.72)
22 centuries, 7 wickets (average: 54.57), 33 catches.
Geoff Boycott was England's most prolific run compiler and also the most single-minded. There were often times when a more adventurous approach would have been more beneficial to his team, but he let nothing detract from his determination to stay at the wicket. Boycott, who wore spectacles in his early career and then contact lenses, made his Test debut as a stubborn right-handed opener against Australia at Trent Bridge in 1964, and at The Oval in the same series he scored the first of his 22 Test centuries. Throughout his career, Boycott courted controversy and was continually in the headlines during a long-running feud with warring factions at Yorkshire where he was both idolized and despised. His highest Test innings of 246 not out against India at Headingly in 1967 did not bring him praise but the temporary loss of his job as England opener because of his snail-like scoring rate. Very much a back foot player, he had a faultless defensive technique and unequalled powers of concentration. Desperately disappointed at being overlooked as England captain,

into self-imposed exile from the Test scene to concentrate on garnering more of his 47,000 runs for Yorkshire. He made a triumphant return to Test cricket in 1977, scoring 107 and 80 not out in his first match against Australia at Trent Bridge. Then on his home ground at Headingley Boycott had his greatest moment in cricket when he became the first player to complete a century of centuries in a Test match on his way to 191. His final Test century came in his 107th match against India at Delhi in 1981. He was then banned in 1982 for joining the rebel tour to South Africa and was never selected by England again despite his well-publicised belief that he was still worthy of a place.

GRAHAM GOOCH
Born: July 23, 1953.
Test record: 59 Tests, 3,746 runs (average: 37.08)
7 centuries, 13 wickets (average: 42.00), 57 catches.
Graham Gooch had the character and determination to overcome the batsman's most dreaded nightmare: a pair in his first Test match. He collected his double duck against the Australians at Edgbaston in 1975. It was his majestic innings of 120 for Essex against Surrey in the 1979 Benson & Hedges Final at Lord's that convinced the cricket world that he was a player of exceptional ability. In the next season against the powerful West Indies he completed his maiden Test century at Lord's. His performances on the 1980-81 tour of West Indies underlined his arrival as an opener worthy of comparison with the greats of the game. He hit 116 in the third Test in Barbados and 153 in the fifth Test in Jamaica, both scores compiled on under-prepared pitches against exceptionally quick and hostile bowling. Gooch, successor to Keith Fletcher as skipper of Essex, was among those banned from Tests for three years for touring South Africa with a 'rebel' side. In his comeback series against Australia in 1985 he produced a magnificent innings of 196 at The Oval. A useful all-rounder who mixes medium-pace bowling with his powerful batting, he opted out of the 1986-87 tour of Australia which let Chris Broad in to be recognised as England's No 1 opener.

DAVID GOWER
Born: April 1, 1957.
Test record: 96 Tests, 6,789 runs (average: 44.66)
14 centuries, 66 catches.
For sheer elegance and artistry, there are few batsmen around today to compare with David Gower. He has great natural talent and has added discipline and concentration to his game in recent years to make himself the complete batsman. He started his first-

class career with Leicestershire in 1975 and was voted Young Cricketer of the Year in 1978. He made his Test debut in the same year and after a successful series against Pakistan, he scored his first Test century against New Zealand at The Oval. By 1979 Gower was the 'golden boy' of English cricket and his 200 not out in the first Test against India at Edgbaston underlined his class and quality. A stylish, relaxed left-handed batsman and a brilliant fielder, Gower has delighted cricket lovers all over the world with his effortless stroking of the ball off both front and back foot. He is vulnerable early in his innings when he tends to be casual and lacking in total concentration. Rested after a series of inconsistent performances, he re-established himself during the 1980-81 visit to the West Indies where the highlight of his tour was a delightful Test innings of 154 not out in Jamaica. He was appointed captain in 1984 but two 5-0 whitewashes by the West Indies sandwiching an Ashes victory over Australia cost him the job. He is always described as 'laid back' but is much more serious and thoughtful about his game than his casual air suggests.

MIKE GATTING
Born: June 6, 1957.
Test record: 58 Tests, 3,563 runs (average: 40.95)
9 centuries, 2 wickets (average: 128.00), 49 catches.
A natural all-round sportsman, Mike Gatting chose cricket rather than soccer as his career and has developed into a determined and capable cricketer, and also an inspiring leader as he proved with his outstanding captaincy of the England team that retained the Ashes in Australia in 1986-87. A graduate from the England schools side, he established himself in the Middlesex team in 1975 but found the transition from County to Test level a difficult one. Despite a satisfactory series against Australia in 1981 he failed to maintain a permanent Test place until the 1984-85 tour of India. He scored his maiden Test century in the Bombay Test, and in the fourth Test at Madras carved a typically determined and aggressive 207. Stocky and pugnacious, he is a compact right-handed batsman who drives and pulls the ball with great power. He is far from graceful and knows his own limitations, but he is an effective forcing batsman who likes to dominate and attack the bowling. He is also a useful medium pace bowler and a capable fielder. His courage is legendary since he insisted on rejoining the West Indies tour in 1985 after returning home for treatment to his nose that had been broken by a Malcolm Marshall bouncer. He again showed typical bulldog spirit and defiance when batting nearly six hours for an unbeaten 150 to prevent Pakistan winning the final Test of a generally disappointing 1987 series.

134

PETER WILLEY
Born: December 6, 1949.
Test record: 26 Tests, 1,184 runs (average: 26.90)
2 centuries, 7 wickets (average: 65.14), 3 catches.
Peter Willey is a determined and capable all-round cricketer, who in the Test arena has been used mainly as a utility player. A solid, defensive right-handed batsman, he whacks the ball with great power when on the attack and is especially effective against pace as he proved at The Oval in 1980 when compiling his first Test century against the West Indies. He shared an unbroken last-wicket stand with Bob Willis that lasted 171 minutes and saved the match for England. He was 100 not out at the close. A man of strong character and blunt opinions, Willey is a handy off-spin bowler who is generally used in a containing role. Despite recurring knee problems, he has been a successful county player for Northamptonshire and a demanding captain of Leicestershire.

IAN BOTHAM
Born: November 24, 1955.
Test record: 94 Tests, 5,057 runs (average: 34.87)
14 centuries, 373 wickets (average: 27.86), 109 catches.
Any man who can walk the length of Britain and Ireland for children's charities, score swashbuckling centuries and send wickets tumbling at the highest level of the game, pilot a 'plane, climb unhurt from crashed cars, march an elephant across the Alps, split a county in a row over the sacking of his pals, present a caring family-man image, and also make the headlines by getting involved in brawls and alleged drug and sex scandals *has* to be a larger than life character. That's a description that sits easily on Botham's broad shoulders. He sounds like the product of a Hollywood scriptwriter with an over-active imagination, but 'Both' is for real and there has been nobody to touch him for enlivening the cricket scene. Few dispute that he is the greatest English-born all-round cricketer ever to swing a bat and a ball. He has taken more Test wickets than any bowler in history and is among England's all-time top ten runmakers. But it's the way that he has got his runs and wickets that has made him a hero of the people. He has done it with a *macho* style and aggression that has made even the staidest of cricket writers reach for new descriptive phrases. His at times seemingly reckless lifestyle has not endeared him to the cricket Establishment, but there is no doubt about who is 'Mr Popularity' with the public—even at his beloved Somerset, the county he left on a matter of principle to join Worcestershire. We should enjoy him while he's here because it will be a long, long time before we see his like again.

JOHN EMBUREY

Born: August 20, 1952.
Test record: 46 Tests, 1027 runs (average: 19.01)
115 wickets (average: 33.52), 28 catches.

By the mid-1980s, John Emburey had taken over the mantle as the world's No 1 off-spinner, but it was a long haul to the top after making his Test debut for England back in 1978. He has not been as prolific a wicket taker as some of his predecessors such as Jim Laker or Fred Titmus, but there have been few to match him for tight, controlled bowling that can squeeze the life out of opposition batsmen. He has a classical action that is right out of the textbook, and his total command of the ball means he can land it on a sixpence. A tall man, he uses his height to get bounce and he is expert at varying the pace and trajectory of his deliveries. He and Phil Edmonds have been a formidable spin team for Middlesex and England. Emburey is a brilliant fielder in the gully, and also a vastly improved late-order batsman who can conjure some swift runs when they are most needed.

BOB TAYLOR

Born: July 17, 1941.
Test record: 57 Tests, 1,156 runs (average: 16.28)
167 catches, 7 stumpings.

There have been few more accomplished wicket keepers than Bob Taylor, who when he at last emerged from the shadow cast by Alan Knott quickly established himself as a worthy successor to Knott behind the stumps for England. A former professional footballer with Port Vale, he enjoyed a career stretching across two decades with Derbyshire for whom he once held 10 catches in a match against Hampshire at Chesterfield in 1963. He set a world record with seven dismissals in an innings and ten in the match against India in the 1980 Golden Jubilee Test in Bombay. Taylor was an absolute purist of a player, unspectacular but totally reliable, and he supplemented his skill behind the stumps with some capable performances with the bat.

GRAHAM DILLEY

Born: May 18, 1959.
Test record: 30 Tests, 391 runs (average: 13.48)
99 wickets (average: 30.02), 9 catches.

Graham Dilley's up-and-down career took off again in spectacular style during the England tour of Australia in 1986-87 when his hostile speed was a vital factor in enabling Mike Gatting's team to retain the Ashes. He lived up to all his early promise when he first started to make an impact with Kent in 1977. His fortunes have swung about like the balls that he bowls and at one stage in the 1980s a combination of illness, injuries, loss of confidence and loss of rhythm seemed to signpost that his England career was over. But this 6 foot 4 inch, 15-stone blond powerhouse showed tremendous character and courage to force his way back to the top and to encourage Worcestershire to offer him a lucrative contract as a partner to Ian Botham, with whom he shared the memorable match-winning seventh wicket stand in the 1981 Headingley Test.

BOB WILLIS
Born: May 30, 1949.
Test record: 90 Tests, 840 runs (average: 11.50)
325 wickets (average: 25.20), 39 catches.
Bob Willis was a born fighter who delighted in proving critics wrong whenever they attempted to write him off during a career hampered by a succession of injuries. A 6 foot 6 inch long-limbed giant, he started his first-class career with Surrey and made his county debut in 1969. He flew out to Australia in 1970-71 as a replacement for injured Alan Ward, and quickly established himself as a key man in the England squad. The following year he joined Warwickshire where, despite his plague of injuries, he continually proved himself one of England's few world-class pace bowlers. He had a run as England captain and motivated his team-mates by example, refusing to admit defeat until the final ball had been bowled. His 325 wickets in 90 Tests was a record overtaken by Ian Botham, with whom he shared the glory in the 1981 Headingley Test with his 8 wickets for 43 in an extra-ordinary spell of 15.1 overs. Strictly a tail-ender, Willis is justly proud of his world record of 55 'not outs' in Test cricket. His highest Test score was 28 – not out, of course.

THEY ALSO SERVED

BOB WOOLMER
Born: May 14, 1948.
Test record: 19 Tests, 1,059 runs (average: 33.09)
3 centuries, 4 wickets (average: 74.75), 10 catches.
Born in Kanpur, India, Bob Woolmer was a talented all-rounder who made 19 Test appearances for England and scored three centuries – all against Australia, two of them in sucessive matches in 1977. He appeared to have become rooted to the pitch when scoring his maiden Test century at The Oval in 1975. It took him six hours 36 minutes, then the slowest in the history of England-Australia Test matches. But he could also score at a cracking pace

as he proved when scoring a century before lunch for Kent against Derbyshire at Chesterfield in 1979. He was a lively medium-fast bowler who performed a hat-trick for MCC against the Australians at Lord's in 1975, and took 7 for 47 for Kent against Sussex in 1979 and in the same season claimed 6 Derbyshire wickets for just 9 runs in a John Player League match. One of the cricketers banned for joining the rebel tour to South Africa, he was forced to retire in 1985 with a recurring back injury.

PAUL DOWNTON
Born: April 4, 1957.
Test record: 27 Tests, 701 runs (average: 19.47)
61 catches, 5 stumpings.
The son of a former Kent wicket keeper, Paul Downton followed in his father's footsteps and briefly took over behind the Kent stumps from one of his heroes, Alan Knott, before switching to Middlesex. It was his batting as much as his efficient wicket keeping that earned him a regular place in the England Test squad. A first-rate Rugby player who has a degree in Law, Downton was good enough with the bat to open for Middlesex with the then England skipper Mike Brearley as his partner. In 1984 he scored his first Test half-century with a battling 56 against West Indies at Edgbaston, and the following season he completed his maiden first-class century while sharing a stand of 289 with Clive Radley for Middlesex against Northants at Lord's.

MIKE HENDRICK
Born: October 22, 1948.
Test record: 30 Tests, 128 runs (average: 6.40)
87 wickets (average: 25.83), 25 catches.
Mike Hendrik wound down his injury-hit career with Nottingham-shire but it's with Derbyshire that his name will always be associated. He was devastating on the quick Derbyshire wickets with his stylish fast-medium bowling, taking 7 for 19 against Hampshire in 1980. In the same season he performed the hat-trick against West Indies at Derby. One of his most startling performances came in a John Player League match at Nottingham in 1972 when he claimed 6 wickets for 7 runs. He made his Test debut in 1974 against India but it was five years before he established himself as an England regular. His best return in his 30 Test matches was 4-28, but that does not reflect his deadly accuracy that continually tied down opposition batsmen. He had a safe pair of hands in the field, particularly close to the wicket and his big swings enlivened many a tail-end run chase.

138

CHRIS OLD

Born: December 22, 1948.
Test record: 46 Tests, 845 runs (average: 14.82)
143 wickets (average: 28.11), 22 catches.

A spirited all-rounder, Chris Old considered himself 'a batsman who could bowl a bit' early in his career with Yorkshire, but gradually his bowling came to the fore and it was with the ball that he made his main reputation as a matchwinner. He took four wickets with five balls for England against Pakistan at Edgbaston in 1978, finishing with 7 for 50. A right-arm fast medium bowler and a hard-hitting left-handed batsman, his best bowling performance for Yorkshire was 7 for 20 against Gloucestershire in 1969. Batting against Warwickshire – the county he joined late in his career – Old scorched to a century in 37 minutes for what was then, in 1977, the second-fastest century in first-class cricket. Yorkshire released him at the end of the 1982 season after he had been captain for one year. The brother of England Rugby Union international Alan Old, Chris was continually hindered by injury throughout his career. He was another of the players banned from the Test arena for joining the rebel tour to South Africa.

CHRIS TAVARE

Born: October 27, 1954.
Test record: 30 Tests, 1,753 runs (average: 33.07)
2 centuries, 20 catches.

A zoologist who studied at Oxford University where he got a cricket blue, Chris Tavare was one of the most stubborn batsmen ever to play for England. He defied and frustrated a procession of bowlers as an opener or No. 3 who always set out to be an anchorman, leaving the eye-catching run-making to batsmen with a wider range of strokes. Tavare was impervious to impatient spectators jeering his slow progress, and unselfishly put the needs of the team above his own personal ambitions. He has shown in several bright knocks for Kent that he can be adventurous but his image as a Test player was always that of a hoarder rather than a chaser of runs.

ALAN KNOTT

Born: April 9, 1946.
Test record: 95 Tests, 4,389 runs (average: 32.75)
5 centuries, 250 catches, 19 stumpings.

In 95 Tests, Alan Knott gave England magnificent service as an agile wicket keeper bouncing with enthusiasm, and also as a batsman who continually came up with vital runs in critical situations. He surpassed the previous records for an England wicket keeper set by Godfrey Evans, his predecessor behind the stumps at Kent. Knott, nicknamed 'The Flea' because of his fanaticism about fitness, made 269 dismissals, holding 250 catches and stumping 19 victims. He was a solid and occasionally spectacular batsman, gathering 4,389 runs for England at an average 32.75. Voted Young Cricketer of the Year in 1965, he made his Test debut against Pakistan two years later. He held the world record for most dismissals until overtaken by Rodney Marsh. His highest Test score was 135 against Australia at Trent Bridge in 1977, one of five battling centuries for England.

PAUL ALLOTT
Born: September 14, 1956.
Test record: 13 Tests, 213 runs (average: 14.20)
26 wickets (average: 41.69), 4 catches.
Paul Allott, powerfully built at 6 foot 4 inches and 14 stone, is a wholehearted right-arm fast-medium bowler who touched his peak in the third Test against the West Indies in 1984 when he took 6 for 61 in the first innings. He was unable to hold down a regular place in the team, but when called on has never let his country down and has swung the bat as well as the ball with great spirit and determination. His outstanding bowling return for Lancashire is 8 for 48 against Northants in 1985.

WAYNE LARKINS
Born : November 22, 1953
Test record: 6 Tests, 176 runs (average: 16.00)
3 catches.
An aggressive right-handed batsman and useful right-arm medium bowler, Wayne Larkins was never able to reproduce his county form in his six Test appearances. He revealed his true ability with his 252 for Northants against Glamorgan at Cardiff in 1983, but this came while he was banned from Test cricket for joining the rebel tour to South Africa. His best bowling performance was 5 for 59 for Northants at Worcester in 1984.

PAUL PARKER
Born: January 15, 1956
Test record: 1 Test, 13 runs (average: 6.50)
Paul Parker, a stylish middle-order batsman with Sussex, has been overlooked by the selectors since his one appearance in the sixth Test against Australia in 1981 when he scored 0 and 13. A Cambridge blue at cricket and Rugby, his top score was 215 for Cambridge against Essex in 1976.

THE TOM GRAVENEY ASSESSMENT

Defeated Australian skipper Kim Hughes said when his nightmare series was over: 'The difference between the two sides was represented by one man and one man only – that man Botham.' In my view, *two* other men should have at least a share in the credit: England captain Mike Brearley and that willing worker of a fast bowler Bob Willis. It was Brearley who on his emergency recall as captain brought order and direction to an England team that under Botham, quite frankly, appeared to lack discipline and professionalism; and it was Willis who did so much to help turn the series with his devastating bowling in the second innings of the Headingley Test. His 8 for 43 return was just reward for one of the most totally committed bowling performances I have ever seen in more than 40 years of playing and watching cricket.

But in the final analysis, the series did belong to Botham who was a new man once the burden of captaincy had been lifted from his shoulders. Just to confirm my feeling that he was better off without the problems of leadership I looked up his personal playing record while skipper and compared it with his form once he was 'a free man'. In the 12 matches in which he captained England his runs totalled just 276 at an average 13.80, with a top score of 57 against the West Indies at Trent Bridge in 1980 in his first Test as skipper. His bowling lost all its snap and he took just 35 wickets at a cost of 32 runs each. In the four remaining Tests against Australia once Brearley had taken over as captain Botham totalled 365 runs, including two unforgettable centuries. He was also back to his tigerish best with the ball, taking 28 wickets. Ian was desperately disappointed to have to surrender the captaincy, but I am sure on this evidence he must concede that without it he could serve both himself and his country better.

It was a remarkable revival by a phenomenal player who looked like a man treading the gangplank towards oblivion when he walked through the Long Room at Lord's to the solitary sound of his own footsteps after collecting his 'pair' in the second Test. What followed was like something out of the pages of *The Wizard* rather than *Wisden*.

Clive Lloyd's West Indies, 1984

> ## THE SQUAD:
>
> Gordon Greenidge (5) Jeff Dujohn (5)   Roger Harper (5)
> Desmond Haynes (5)   Clive Lloyd (5)   Joel Garner (5)
> Larry Gomes (5)   Malcolm Marshall (4) Milton Small (1)
> Vivian Richards (5)   Eldine Baptise (5)   Winston Davis (1)
>   Michael Holding (4)
>
> ### SCOREBOARD: 5 Tests, 5 victories
>
> *Figures in brackets indicate the number of Test match appearances*

BACKGROUND

Clive Lloyd's 1984 West Indies—*the Whirlwinding Windies*—blasted through England with a speed and style never before witnessed. They created a unique record by becoming the first overseas team in cricket history to win all five Tests in a series in England. It was a total whitewash; or, as a banner brandished by ecstatic West Indian supporters at The Oval during the final Test put it: 'BLACKWASH!'

A 5-0 result had been recorded only four times before in 107 years of Test cricket: by Australia against England in 1920-21 and against South Africa in 1931-32; England against India in 1959, and Frank Worrell's West Indies against India in 1961-62. Two things are vital for a team bidding to win all five Tests in a series —one, a dry summer enabling uninterrupted play; two, a side of all-round playing strength and skill. The summer of 1984 was dry and far too hot for England, and the West Indies team did not have a single weakness in any department.

They batted all the way down to No 10, with Gordon Greenidge, Larry Gomes, Clive Lloyd and the incomparable Viv Richards all averaging over 40 during a never-ending run riot against the outgunned England attack. In Jeff Dujon they had a gymnastic wicket keeper whose run-gathering average of 35 was higher over the five-Test series than that achieved by all but one England batsman. They had a first-rate off-spinner in Roger Harper, and a battery of exceedingly quick and deadly fast bowlers who, in more ways than one, played with great bounce and confidence: Michael Holding, Malcolm Marshall and the giant Joel Garner, supported by the lively fast-medium-pace of all-rounder Eldine Baptiste.

TOM GRAVENEY: 'We thought long and hard before selecting this team as the representatives of the cluster of outstanding sides that Clive Lloyd led during his record run of 74 matches as West Indies captain. They just edged out Clive's 1976 team that blitzed Tony Greig's England 3-0 following Tony's ill-advised "We'll make them grovel" prophecy. The 1984 team had everything, from blinding pace to batting of the highest order and also telling spin from Roger Harper. Their fielding was quite electric, and there was never any sign of the sort of temperamental frailties that had tripped up West Indian teams in the past. You can usually pick out two or three obvious matchwinners from each Test series, but this West Indies team had a whole host of them – a master for every moment. I have to say that I thought the West Indians were allowed to overdo the intimidating, short-pitch bowling tactic against England batsmen who were often torn between the instinct of defending themselves and the duty of defending their wicket. It was I felt particularly unwarranted when Malcolm Marshall was trying to bounce out nightwatchman Percy Pocock in the final Test at The Oval. Pocock was strictly a tail-ender, and it left a bad taste in the mouth to see him being given the sort of hostile treatment that, if it has to be introduced at all, should be reserved for established batsmen. It was nasty and it was unnecessary from a team that in all other respects was just about irresistible.'

THE OPPOSITION

David Gower had been given the captaincy of an England team trying to reassert itself after tour defeats in Pakistan and New Zealand. He was shorn of the services of established front-line players like Geoff Boycott, Graham Gooch, John Lever and Derek Underwood because of their TCCB ban for joining in the rebel tour of South Africa. If ever England needed their strongest team in action it was in this series against a West Indies side fresh from trouncing Australia 3-0. Gower could not have taken over at a more demanding time, and he could have done without the selectors experimenting by giving five players their first taste of

143

Test cricket: Andy Lloyd, Chris Broad, Paul Terry, Jonathan Agnew and Richard Ellison. It was experience rather than experimentation that was needed. For Lloyd and Terry it was a nightmare introduction to the international arena. Both were put out of action for the rest of the season after being injured by balls that became lethal weapons in the hands of the West Indian pace bowlers. Worst of all for Gower was that he could not answer fire with fire. Bob Willis was coming to the end of the line as a strike bowler who had given his all for England, and the likes of Ian Botham, David Pringle and Paul Allott just did not have the speed to match the West Indians. The England selectors threw 21 players into battle over the five-Test series, but it was quality that was needed rather than quantity.

THE TEST MATCHES
FIRST TEST: Edgbaston (June 14-18)

David Gower won the toss and elected to bat, a decision that was met with raised eyebrows by locals who knew that the wicket would in the early stages be at its juiciest after recent rain. They were conditions conducive to speed – and the West Indians have that aplenty! The result was five England wickets down before lunch, and one of them a near-tragedy. Debutant opener Andy Lloyd, the first Shropshire-born cricketer to represent England in a home Test, was hit on the side of the head by a sharply rising ball from Malcolm Marshall and was taken off to hospital where he spent eight days under supervision because of blurred vision. Only the bold Botham (64) and wicket keeper Paul Downton (33) played the fast bowlers with any real conviction and England were rushed all out for 191, with the giant Joel Garner (4-53) the most successful with the ball. The West Indian batsmen then proceeded to prove they were every bit as brilliant as the bowlers. They were batting half an hour after tea on the first day and over the next ten hours amassed a mountain of 606 runs. Larry Gomes (143) and Viv Richards (117) led the assault on an England attack in which Pringle had five wickets to show for his 108-run battering. The careful, constructive Gomes shared a third wicket stand of 206 with the imperious Richards and a fifth wicket stand of 124 with skipper Clive Lloyd (71). England thought they were at last making a vital breakthrough when they were held up by a barnstorming ninth wicket stand of 150 in 113 minutes by Eldine Baptiste (87 not out) and Michael Holding (69). Downton was promoted to open the England second innings in the absence of the injured Andy Lloyd and he beavered away for a top score

144

Ian Botham bowls against Australia in the 1981 Headingley Test (left) and celebrates his 300th Test wicket against West Indies at The Oval in 1984.

Australian skipper Allan Border looks on from the slips as Ian Botham powers
the ball to the boundary in the Melbourne Test in 1986.

Above: Bob Willis on a glory run after his 8 for 43 had helped clinch England's victory over Australia at Headingley in 1981.

Right: Field marshal Mike Brearley dictates the pattern of play during the unforgettable 1981 Headingley Test.

Mike Gatting, a dominant batsman and an inspiring team leader who succeeded David Gower as England skipper in 1986.

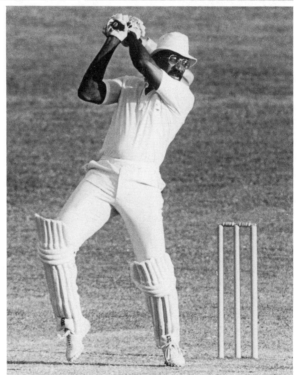

Viv Richards (top, left), Gordon Greenidge (top, right) and Clive Lloyd (right) helped lay the foundation of runs on which the West Indies built their incredible success in the 1980s.

Michael Holding, an artist in his approach but violent with his delivery, in action for West Indies at The Oval where he took 14 England wickets in 1976.

Joel Garner, the 'Big Bird' of the West Indies who swoops for his wickets, was the most effective bowler in the 1984 series in England with 27 wickets.

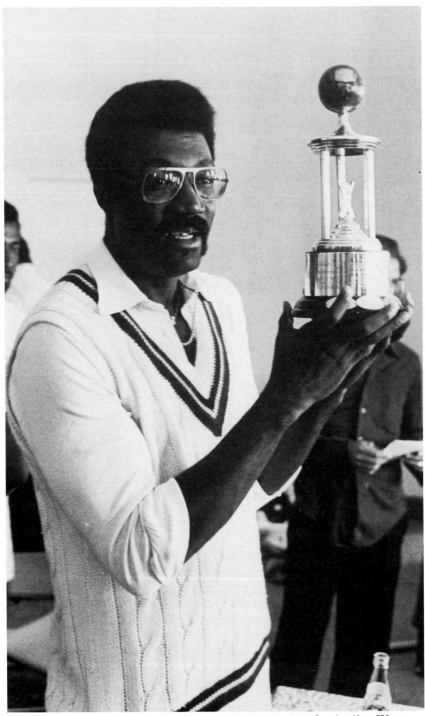

Clive Lloyd holds the treasured Sir Frank Worrell trophy after leading West Indies to victory in the 1980 Test series in Australia.

of 56 as England struggled to avoid an ignominious innings defeat against a hostile West Indies attack in which Garner (5-55) was again the main menace. Pringle (46 not out) and Botham (38) caused a slight delay to the inevitable victory for West Indies, and Botham managed to unsettle Marshall to the extent where he was warned by umpire Dickie Bird for intimidating bowling. Botham being intimidated? That seems hardly possible, but there were many neutral onlookers at that Test series in the summer of 1984 who felt the umpires should have handed out a lot more warnings for West Indian bowling that was sometimes vicious and often bordered on the violent. **RESULT: West Indies (606) beat England (191 and 235) by an innings and 180 runs.**

SECOND TEST: Lord's (June 28-July 3)

England were put into bat and got off to a promising start in this centenary of Tests at the headquarters of cricket. Graeme Fowler (106) and debutant Chris Broad (55) – the seventh different openers paired by the selectors in eight matches – produced a century stand that was ended when Broad was caught down the leg side by wicket keeper Jeff Dujon to give Malcolm Marshall the first of his six wickets for 85. Botham scored a rapid 30 in a respectable England total of 286 and then excelled with the ball, taking 8 for 103 to help dismiss West Indies for 245. Botham included his Somerset pal Viv Richards (72) among his victims, one of a record-equalling 12 players given out during the match to an lbw decision. For the one and only time in the series England were on top and Allan Lamb (110) and Botham (81) piled on the runs against an attack missing the services of the injured Michael Holding. His stand-in, Milton Small, was the most effective of the West Indian fast bowlers in the second innings with 3 for 40. Gower declared at 300 for 9 after 20 minutes' play on the final day, leaving West Indies with a mammoth victory target of 341. Well it *looked* mammoth on paper, but Gordon Greenidge (214 not out) and Larry Gomes (92 not out) knocked off the runs with incredible ease after Desmond Haynes had been run out with the score at 57. It was the first time West Indies had lost a second innings wicket in seven matches. Their unbroken partnership of 287 was a new second wicket record in England-West Indies Tests. Greenidge included 29 fours and two sixes on his way to becoming the first West Indian to score a double century at Lord's. It was the first time since 1948 that England had lost after declaring their second innings closed, a fact that achieved little for Gower's peace of mind. **RESULT: West Indies (245 and 344-1) beat England (286 and 300) by 9 wickets.**

THIRD TEST: Headingley (July 12-16)

The bowling and bravery of Malcolm Marshall and the batting of Larry Gomes lifted West Indies to an emphatic victory and clinched the retention of the Wisden Trophy by the early afternoon of the fourth day. A second successive century by Allan Lamb and another solid knock by Ian Botham (45) put England in a strong position at 237 for 6 but the tail folded and they were all out for 270. Lancashire strike bowler Paul Allott (6-61) proved the selectors right to recall him after two years in the wilderness with a superb spell that at last took the weight off Bob Willis who was playing in his 90th and final Test. Michael Holding (59) gave Willis a painful send-off by striking five sixes in his tail-end blast in support of the immoveable Gomes (104 not out). Gomes was still short of his century when last-man Malcolm Marshall came to the wicket to bat one handed after fracturing his left thumb stopping a shot from Chris Broad on the first morning.This bought time for Gomes to reach his second 100 of the series and Marshall managed to swat the ball one-handed to the boundary for four before Botham caught him off Allott's bowling to close the West Indies innings at 302. Marshall, ignoring medical advice that he should drop out of the match, did not allow the plaster on his left hand to handicap him and his 7-53 sent England reeling to a second innings total of 159, with only Graeme Fowler (50) and David Gower (43) salvaging reasonable scores. Gordon Greenidge (49) and Desmond Haynes (43) shared an opening stand of 106 to send West Indies on the way to victory by eight wickets. Bob Willis bowed out at the end of his great Test career with two records to his name: an English record 325 Test wickets (since overtaken by Botham) and a world record of 55 'not out' innings. **RESULT: West Indies (302 and 131-2) beat England (270 and 159) by 8 wickets.**

FOURTH TEST: Old Trafford (July 26-31)

Gordon Greenidge laid the foundation for another decisive West Indies victory with his second double century of the series. His 223 – supported by Jeff Dujon (101) and Malcolm Marshall's deputy Winston Davis (77) – helped West Indies to a grand total of 500 after Allott had given England an early boost by removing Larry Gomes, Viv Richards and Clive Lloyd in the space of 13 deliveries. Pat (Percy) Pocock, making his Test comeback after eight years at the age of 37, bowled a marathon 45.3 overs and was rewarded for his labours with 4 for 121. Graeme Fowler (38) and Chris Broad (42) gave England another sound start but

146

then only Allan Lamb with a rare third successive Test century stood firm as England collapsed to 280 all out. Paul Terry had his left arm broken by a ball from Winston Davis. Terry retired hurt and then at the fall of the ninth wicket, following confusion as to whether or not the England innings was over, he returned to bat one-handed while Lamb completed his century. Joel Garner (4-51) and Eldine Baptiste (3-31) were the most effective of the West Indian bowlers. Clive Lloyd enforced the follow on and Holding bowled Fowler before a run had been scored. Despite a captain's innings by David Gower (57 not out) England surrendered, this time to the spin of Roger Harper (6-57). They were all out for 156 at just after mid-day on the final day. **RESULT: West Indies (500) beat England (280 and 156) by an innings and 64 runs.**

FIFTH TEST: The Oval (August 9-14)

England looked as if they might salvage some self-respect with a victory in the final Test when the West Indies tumbled to 70 for 6 against some inspired bowling by Ian Botham (5-72). His first three victims – key men Gordon Greenidge, Viv Richards and Jeff Dujon – took him to 300 wickets in Test cricket and he became the first player to complete the double of 3,000 runs and 300 wickets. But celebrations for Botham were quickly mooted by a fight back led by Clive Lloyd (60 not out) and the last four wickets contributed 120 for a total of 190. England were at last looking at a West Indies total that was more of a hill than a mountain, but a hostile spell of bowling by Malcolm Marshall (5-35) turned their reply into a relative molehill. They were all out for 162, with Fowler top scorer on 31 in a two-phase innings after retiring with a bruised forearm when a Marshall thunderbolt struck him. Many people thought that Marshall went beyond the boundaries of fair play when he also sent a string of bouncers zipping around the head of nightwatchman Percy Pocock, who during the match became the first England player this century to be dismissed for a 'pair' twice in consecutive matches. That sad statistic plus Marshall missiles whizzing past his ears was more than the popular Surrey veteran deserved. Desmond Haynes (125) found his form after a sterile series and along with Jeff Dujon (49) and skipper Lloyd (36) pushed the West Indies second innings total up to a solid 346. England needed 375 to win or to bat for ten hours to save the match, but these distant targets disappeared from sight when Michael Holding (5-43) unleashed his fastest spell of the series to dismiss Chris Broad, David Gower and Allan Lamb in the space of 17 balls and for just five runs. Chris Tavare (49) batted with typical grit and Botham

(54) with typical dash but it was all to no avail and Joel Garner (4-51) finished off the England innings and the chillingly one-sided series a minute after noon on the final day. **RESULT: West Indies (190 and 346) beat England (162 and 202) by 172 runs.**

THE CAPTAIN

All the facts and figures point to Clive Lloyd having been the most successful skipper in the history of Test cricket. He was captain for a record 74 matches from 1974 until his retirement from the international stage in 1985 after 110 Test appearances. West Indies won 36, lost 12 and drew 26 of the matches under his leadership. Seven of those defeats were sustained during his first 13 Tests as skipper, five of them in his rock-bottom series against Lillee-and-Thomson inspired Australia in 1975-76 when many experienced cricket watchers wondered whether he was out of his depth as a Test captain.

But 'Big Cat' as he was affectionately known grew with the job, and he proved that he was able to shoulder the responsibility by giving improved performances as a player. His run-making average increased from 38.67 in 36 matches before becoming captain to 51.30 in his 74 matches as the man in charge.

Lloyd, born in Georgetown, Guyana in 1944, made his bow for the West Indies against India in 1966 and in his debut scored 82 and 78 not out. He then purred to a century in his first appearance against England and also scored a hundred in his debut against Australia, giving an early indication of the strong will-power and steely determination that lay just below the surface of a seemingly easy-going, laid-back attitude to cricket and to life. He was an immensely powerful yet at the same time elegant left-handed batsman, and – before a recurring knee injury restricted his mobility – a potent right-arm medium-pace bowler and a fielder capable of miracles in the covers.

His dynamic hitting and contagious enthusiasm for every aspect of the game turned him into an idol of Lancashire with whom he had a warm 16-year association including a successful spell as captain from 1981. He will always be remembered for a whole gallery of great innings including his unbeaten 217 for Lancashire against Warwickshire at Old Trafford in 1971, an unbeaten 242 for West Indies against India in Bombay in 1974-75, a hurricane 200 in 120 minutes for West Indies against Glamorgan at Swansea in 1976, and a procession of thrilling knocks for West Indies in one-day internationals. A lot of people made the error of mistaking his genial personality for meaning that he was too soft, but he could crack down as a tough

148

disciplinarian when it mattered, and he was never afraid of standing up for himself against the Establishment. He met the West Indies Board of Control head-on in the world-wide bust up over the Kerry Packer revolution and became a leading member of World Series Cricket before being welcomed back into the West Indies fold with open arms by Board officials who realized that they needed him more than he needed them.

A stooping, gangling giant of a man with distinctive spectacles and a long, loping stride, Lloyd had great presence on and off the pitch and throughout his career was one of the most easily recognizable and popular cricketers on the world circuit. Called Hubert – his second name – by many people, he was the cousin of top West Indies spin bowler Lance Gibbs. He never used to build innings for the sake of it, but always with a purpose. It was the needs of the team that were uppermost in his mind and he used to set the pace and pattern of matches with his batting and his shrewd field placings and intelligent bowling changes. *Test record:* 110 Tests, 7,515 runs (average: 46.67), 19 centuries. Captain in 74 Tests (36 wins, 12 defeats, 26 draws).

TOM GRAVENEY: 'I have good reason to remember Clive's Test debut against England. It was in the opening Test at Port-of-Spain in 1967-68 with Gary Sobers as skipper for the first time. In the first innings I managed to score 118 in a fourth wicket stand of 188 with that marvellous battler Ken Barrington. I got lucky in the slips when West Indies replied and held on to catches from openers Seymour Nurse and Steve Camacho and also the great Sobers. But the big left-handed newcomer Lloyd handled our attack like a master and I recall saying to our captain Colin Cowdrey alongside me in the slips, "Skip, he's going to give a lot of our bowlers stick in the years to come." Clive scored 118, exactly the same total as me, and – despite an occasional weakness against real speed – he did indeed give England and all the world's cricketing nations stick over the next 17 years or so. When he was really flowing there were few better sights in cricket than Lloyd at the wicket, as anybody who witnessed his spectacular matchwinning century for West Indies in the World Cup Final at Lord's in 1975 will testify. There were times when he could be careless and impetuous and tempted into going for shots best left in the locker, but when he was really timing the ball he had the strokes and the style to take any attack apart with a savagery that provided a wonderful spectacle for everybody but the bowlers and the fielders on the receiving end. Of course, his biggest impact was as captain of a succession of exceptionally talented teams that revolutionized the way the game of cricket is played. When I first came into the game you could bank on a Test side consisting of a couple of quickies, a medium-pacer and two spinners. West Indies under Lloyd's leadership often used to go into battle without even bothering with a spinner. The emphasis was on pace, pace and still more pace and like all his predecessors he could call on a vast array of super batsmen to give his bowlers plenty of runs to play with. It speaks volumes for Lloyd's steadying influence as captain that he was able to have such a stable team. It is interesting to note that he needed to call on only 44 players throughout his run of 74 matches in charge. Over the same period England's selectors called up 74 players!

He had the total respect of his players, but there were times when perhaps he should have exercised greater on-field discipline. It could get quite nasty out in the middle when his strike bowlers were overdoing the short-pitched stuff and literally putting lives in danger with an overload of bouncers. Clive, for all his warmth and friendliness off the pitch, was a man who liked to win and he knew just how to use the most aggressive tactics to make sure that more times than not West Indies came out on top.'

THE PLAYERS

GORDON GREENIDGE
Born: May 1, 1951.
Test record: 74 Tests, 5,165 runs (average: 47.38)
12 centuries, 68 catches.

Gordon Greenidge exploded on to the Test scene in India in 1974, celebrating his first Test with scores of 93 and 107. Two years later after a disasterous tour of Australia he went into the series in England determined to prove he was back on top as West Indies' No. 1 opener. He proceeded to carve three centuries and two half-centuries in the five-match rubber and firmly established himself as the best foundation-builder in the business. Gordon is possibly the perfect product for world cricket: Barbados-born with all the inherent gifts of a West Indian strokemaker, and with the disciplines of the English game instilled into him from the age of 14 when his parents emigrated to Berkshire. He played for England schoolboys and was snapped up by Hampshire in 1968, but it was with his native West Indies that he decided to play his Test cricket. There has rarely, if ever, been a right-hand opening bat to match him for the power with which he hits the ball. He likes to dominate the bowling as early as possible in his innings with a repetoire of shots more usually associated with a carefree No. 3 or No. 4 batsman. He drives, cuts, hooks and pulls with

great ferocity and perfect timing. He occasionally suffers from
loss of concentration and is at his most vulnerable in the early
stages of his innings. But once he gets anchored at the crease he
can become immoveable as he proved with his two double
centuries against England in the 1984 Test series. He is prone to
injury and illness, but the sight of an allegedly half-fit Greenidge
limping to the wicket fills bowlers and fielders with despair
because he is as dangerous as a wounded lion and invariably
produces his finest knocks when less than 100 per cent fit. He
was enormously influenced early in his career at Hampshire by
South African master Barry Richards. Once Richards had retired
he became a more mature and responsible player, yet continued to
produce the flowing shots that Barry had encouraged him to
cultivate. Among his devastating displays for Hampshire was a
knock of 259 against Sussex in 1975, 136 and 120 against Kent
in 1978, and a remarkable 163 not out in a John Player League
match in 1979, a hurricane innings that was studded with 10
sixes. Greenidge has conquered vision problems by adjusting to
spectacles and now stands unchallenged as the world's premier
opening batsman.

DESMOND HAYNES
Born: February 15, 1956.
Test record: 62 Tests, 3,852 runs (average: 42.32)
 8 centuries, 39 catches.
Desmond Haynes became a running mate to Gordon Greenidge
after a stop-start commencement to his Test career that was interrupted by his exile with World Series Cricket. He made his Test
debut against Australia in 1978 and got off to a promising start
by scoring 61, 66 and 55 in his first two Test matches. An
attacking batsman by nature, Haynes developed into a solid and
dependable right-handed opening batsman who controlled his
desire to go for flashy hooks until well set at the wicket. He
proved his big-match temperament by gathering 184 runs in the
Lord's Test on the 1980 tour of England during which he
averaged 46.00 runs in all matches and an impressive 51.33 in
the Tests. Tall and stylish, his batting technique and role of
anchorman triggers memories of his distinguished predecessor as
West Indies and Barbados opener, Conrad Hunte. He can compile runs patiently in the tradition of conventional openers or can
quicken the tempo by producing an array of risky but spectacular
attacking shots. He was having a miserable tour of England in
1984 and was completely overshadowed by Greenidge and Larry
Gomes, but when these two failed for once to come up with vital
runs in the final Test he revealed his stunning talent with a

matchwinning century. Haynes, an excellent fielder and an occasional right-arm leg-break and googly bowler, topped the batting averages against England in 1985-86 with 78.16.

LARRY GOMES
Born: July 13, 1953.
Test record: 57 Tests, 3,099 runs (average: 40.77)
9 centuries, 13 wickets (average: 66.69), 17 catches.

Fifteen successive innings without a half-century to his name seemed to have signposted the end of the Test career of Larry Gomes. He was dropped from the team tor the 1983-84 series against Australia in favour of young Antiguan Richie Richardson, and when he was included in the party for the England tour most people thought it would be as a back-up member of the squad. The 30-year-old Trinidadian quietly went into the nets before embarking on the tour and worked on a change of style, facing a bowling machine for hours on end while trying out a new grip that forced him to play straight instead of across the line of the flight. He emerged from the practice sessions virtually a new batsman and grew in stature from the moment the tour to England started. Less demonstrative and spectactular than many of his batting colleagues, left-handed Gomes carefully accumulated runs with a determination that frustrated a battery of bowlers. His form in the Tests was a revelation, completing two centuries and finishing second in the batting averages only to Gordon Greenidge with a remarkable 80.00. Gomes, one of five cricketing brothers, is enormously popular in his native Trinidad where he coaches the army of young players dreaming of following in his footsteps.When he was left out of the West Indies party for the 1980 tour of England, club cricketers in Trinidad wore black arm bands in protest. After his magnificent performances against England four years later he was given the accolade of being named one of the five *Wisden* Cricketers of the Year.

VIV RICHARDS
Born: March 7, 1952.
Test record: 85 Tests, 6,395 runs (average: 53.73)
20 centuries, 20 wickets (average: 53.05), 80 catches.

You would have to go a long, long way to find a greater batsman than Isaac Vivian Alexander Richards, perhaps out of the galaxy! He is that rarity among cricketing men: a classically orthodox batsman who is always looking to be unconventional and inventive. From the moment of his earliest runs in his native Antigua Richards could bat with the rhythm, grace and power that comes only to a natural born genius. No textbook or coach could have taught him the timing and flair of his strokes that was evident in his play from the moment he first made an impact with the Leeward Isles in the early 1970s when only his temperament threatened his march towards Test team recognition. He was suspended for two years at the age of 17 for disputing a decision and causing a near-riot among his supporters. It was a sharp shock for him, and his behaviour has since been exemplary and a credit to the teachings of his father, Malcolm Richards, a one-time leading fast bowler in Antigua who encouraged his three sons to follow in his sporting footsteps. Like his two brothers, Viv was an exceptional footballer but—whether batting, bowling off-spin or fielding close to the wicket or in the covers—cricket was always his first love. His career really took off when he joined Somerset in 1974, the start of a mutually sweet and successful 12-year association that was soured only in the last months. In his early days at Somerset he came under the intoxicating influence of former England skipper Brian Close, and he and a young team-mate called Ian Botham started to bring cricketing excitement and entertainment to the cider county. Seemingly relaxed at the wicket almost to the point of sleeping, Richards is always wide awake when there are runs to be plundered and he assembled five double centuries for Somerset among his procession of memorable innings. He proved he had blossomed into a Test batsman of incomparable class during the 1976 West Indies tour of England when he averaged an incredible 118.42 in the Test series. In eight months of that year he harvested 1,710 Test runs at an average 90.00 which is a record for a calendar year. Four years later he hammered the England attack for an average 63.16 runs in the Test series, and was relatively restrained in the 1984 series with an average of 'only' 41.66. He has gathered hundreds of runs all over the world in all conditions and in all climates, and he continues to dominate bowling attacks like only the greats such as Sir Don Bradman and Sir Jack Hobbs have been able to do.

Richards played in 70 of the 74 Tests in which Clive Lloyd was skipper and in 1985 took on the awesome task of succeeding Clive as captain. The extra responsibility did not appear to have an anchoring effect on his genius and in 1986 he led West Indies to a second successive 5-0 'blackwash' of England and he finished second in the batting averages with 66.20. He included the fastest century in Test history in his gallery, smashing six sixes and seven fours on his way to 100 off just 56 balls. Richards joined the village team of Rishton in 1987 and brought the sunshine of his style to the Lancashire League.

JEFF DUJON
Born: May 28, 1956.
Test record: 40 Tests, 1,876 runs (average: 38.28)
 4 centuries, 130 catches, 3 stumpings.
Jeff Dujon won a place in the West Indies Test team on the 1981-82 tour of Australia on the strength of his batting alone, and after topping 40 in each of his first four innings was selected for the third Test as keeper-batsman in succession to David Murray. Agile and reliable behind the stumps, Dujon cemented his place in the team with a succession of outstanding middle-order batting displays including a maiden Test century against India in Antigua in 1982-83. He was top scorer with 130 in the second Test against Australia in Trinidad in 1983-84 and completed his third Test century against England at Old Trafford in 1984. Dujon, whose consistent batting and safe, reliable wicket keeping with Jamaica has been a feature of Shell competition matches, was restored as No. 1 West Indies keeper after injury cost him his place in the second Test against England in 1985-86.

MALCOLM MARSHALL
Born: April 18, 1958.
Test record: 48 Tests, 985 runs (average: 18.58)
 231 wickets (average: 21.23), 23 catches.
Malcolm Marshall had by the mid-1980s established himself as the quickest of the battery of West Indian strike bowlers – which meant he was the fastest man in the world. His 24 wickets in the 1984 series against England was a key factor in the 5-0 victory and he followed this with 27 wickets at an average 17.85 in the 1985-86 series in the West Indies. He made a sensational start to his first-class career, taking 6 for 77 for Barbados against Jamaica at Bridgetown in the 1977-78 Shell Shield match and was selected for the West Indies tour of India on the evidence of this one performance. Hampshire signed Marshall and he became one of the most feared bowlers on the County circuit with the sort of fierce and hostile bowling that has unnerved a long queue of batsmen around the world. He has a whippy action and his short-pitched deliveries have often brought accusations of dangerous gamesmanship. His powerful right-hand batting makes him a superior late-order batsman.

ELDINE BAPTISTE
Born: March 12, 1960.
Test record: 9 Tests, 224 runs (average: 24.88)
15 wickets (average: 32.40), 2 catches.
A powerful middle-order right-handed batsman and lively fast-

medium bowler, Eldine Baptiste was voted the outstanding schoolboy prospect in his native Antigua in 1979 and two years later started a successful association with Kent. He has been a consistent all-rounder for the Leeward Isles in Shell Shield matches and provided excellent support to the West Indies main strike bowlers in the 1984 Test series in England. His 87 not out in a record ninth wicket stand with Michael Holding helped West Indies to their innings victory over England in the first 1984 Test.

ROGER HARPER
Born: March 17, 1963.
Test record: 19 Tests, 352 runs (average: 16.00)
 40 wickets (average: 27.25), 24 catches.
Roger Harper is widely recognized as the finest West Indian off-spinner since the reign of Lance Gibbs. He has been unlucky to be at his peak in an era when pace is king, but he has still managed to make an impressive impact with his clever flight and vicious spin. His performance against England in the 1984 Old Trafford Test when he took 6 for 57 proved that spin could still win matches. He is a first-rate fielder and a competent batsman as he revealed when scoring 127 for Northants against Kent at Maidstone in 1985. Both he and his brother have been key players for Guyana in Shell Shield matches.

MICHAEL HOLDING
Born: February 16, 1954.
Test record: 59 Tests, 910 runs (average: 14.00)
249 wickets (average: 23.28), 21 catches.
There have been few more beautiful sights in modern cricket than that of Michael Holding running in to bowl with his graceful, rhythmic action. It came as almost a shock to the system that this smooth, artistic approach to the wicket could produce such violent deliveries that for a decade left some of the greatest batsmen in the world playing and missing and often listening to that unwelcome sound of falling timber. Nobody who saw him in full flow during the 1976 Test series in England could doubt that they were watching one of the all-time great fast bowlers. He skittled England for 71 at Old Trafford with 5 for 17 on a treacherous pitch, and at The Oval on a featherbed wicket took 8 for 92 and 14 for 149 in the match with as magnificent a sustained spell of speed bowling as ever seen at that famous old ground. He was considerably slower but equally accurate in the 1984 series against England and took 15 wickets. Brilliant with the ball and sometimes surprising with the bat for Jamaica, Lancashire and then Derbyshire, he was one of the most feared yet at the same

time respected bowlers on the international scene until bowing out of Test cricket in 1987.

JOEL GARNER
Born: December 16, 1952.
Test record: 56 Tests, 661 runs (average: 12.96)
247 wickets (average: 21.16), 39 catches.

Pounding in to bowl in his size 16 custom-built boots, the 6 foot 8 inch, 17-stone giant Joel Garner is a terrifying sight for batsmen waiting for him to deliver the ball at an extremely quick pace that invariably induces high bounce on even docile pitches. Nicknamed 'Big Bird', he made many successful swoops in the 1984 series and finished as top wicket taker with 27 at an average 18.62. He was equally effective in the return series in the West Indies in 1985-86 when he again claimed 27 wickets, this time at an average 16.14. A genial giant until out in the middle as a determined competitor, he is no mug with the bat as he proved with a century for the West Indies against Gloucestershire in 1980. Skipper of the Barbados side that won the Shell Shield in 1986, he had the bitter disappointment the same year of hearing that his services were no longer required at Somerset where he had been a popular and prolific performer since 1977.

THEY ALSO SERVED

MILTON SMALL
Born: February 12, 1964.
Test record: 2 Tests, 3 runs, 4 wickets (average: 38.25).

Milton Small toured England in 1984 as a support bowler and was required only for the second Test as deputy for injured Michael Holding. He shared the new ball with his fellow-Barbadian Joel Garner, taking 0 for 38 off nine overs in the first innings and 3 for 40 off 12 overs in the second innings.

WINSTON DAVIS
Born: September 18, 1958.
Test record: 9 Tests, 141 runs (average: 23.50)
22 wickets (average: 40.63), 6 catches.

Winston Davis was recruited from Glamorgan to replace injured Malcolm Marshall in the fourth Test of the 1984 series. He proved almost as deadly as Marshall, breaking Paul Terry's arm with a ball during a spell in the first innings in which he took 2 for 71. His greatest contribution to the West Indies victory was with the bat when he made a career-best 77. Davis switched from Glamorgan to Northants in 1987.

156

THE TOM GRAVENEY ASSESSMENT

David Gower must wonder what he did to upset the cricketing gods that ten of his 26 matches as captain of England were against Clive Lloyd's West Indies. The fact that England set a record best kept in the chamber of horrors by losing every one of the matches for two successive 'blackwashes' underlines why we selected the 1984 West Indies for inclusion in this debate as to which has been the greatest of the great Test teams.

Uneven pitches and questionable batting techniques partially explained why England caved in so pathetically, as did the absence because of the South African issue of banned players of the calibre of Geoff Boycott, Graham Gooch and Derek Underwood. But no matter who went out in an England cap—or should I say helmet?—to face the West Indies I feel they would have been swept aside by Clive Lloyd's hurricane force.

Lloyd based his tactics on sheer aggression and had the players, with the bat and the ball, to carry out his 'blitzkreig' orders. At times it was not a pretty sight to see the battery of West Indian fast bowlers digging the ball in so short that I was literally in fear for the life of some of our batsmen who didn't appear to have the first idea how to cope with the rising ball. England's fast bowlers were a yard or more slower than their Caribbean counterparts and it became almost embarrasing to see the ease with which the likes of Gordon Greenidge, Larry Gomes and Viv Richards played them when compared with how our batsmen struggled.

To be honest, England were outclassed in every department of the game by a team that has amassed overwhelming evidence to support them as the greatest of all time in the final argument. I just wish they had not achieved their success with such vicious intent. They could have conquered England just as emphatically without needing to introduce their tactics of terror that I feel have no place in the Test arena. In the time-honoured phrase, it's just not cricket!

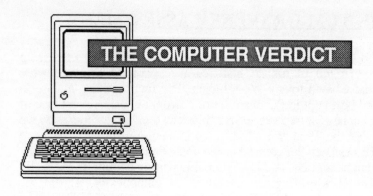

All available facts and figures about the teams featured in this **Ten Greatest Test Teams** *argument—the players and their performances—were fed into a computer, and we present a player-by-player breakdown of the findings on the following pages. As well as overall team achievements, the factors taken into account included all individual batting and bowling averages, Test match experience, fielding ability, the compilation of centuries, competitiveness, flair, and all-rounder powers. Each player was also given computer points for match-winning influence, and this is indicated in the team tables that follow by cricket-ball symbols alongside each name. Only four players collected the maximum number of ten cricket balls: Don Bradman, Garfield Sobers, Dennis Lillee and Ian Botham. There was also a captaincy factor taken into consideration, with computer assessments made on the basis of, among other things, tactical skill, motivating powers, team results and general leadership qualities. We also added feelings to the facts and figures, allowing for instance that Ali Bacher's team was short on Test experience because of South Africa's ban from Test cricket since 1970. The computer was programmed to accept that players of the calibre of Barry Richards, Graeme Pollock and Mike Procter were far superior to what was suggested by their handful of Test matches. Each player was assessed as if at the peak of his ability. If you disagree with the findings blame the computer which was programmed by English cricket lovers who tried very hard to bury any bias towards English heroes.*

BRADMAN'S 1948 Australians

Sidney Barnes
13T 1072r (63.05) 1 100; 4w (54.50), 14c   *RATING: 77*

Arthur Morris
46T 3533r (46.48) 12 100s; 2w (25.00), 15c   *RATING: 79*

Don Bradman
52T 6996r (99.94) 29 100s; 2w (36.00), 32c   *RATING: 98*

Lindsay Hassett
43T 3073r (46.56) 10 100s; 0w (78.00), 30c   *RATING: 84*

Keith Miller
55T 2958r (36.97) 7 100s; 170w (22.97), 38c   *RATING: 94*

Sam Loxton
12T 544r (36.93) 1 100; 8w (43.62), 7c   *RATING: 50*

Ian Johnson
45T 1000r (18.51); 109w (29.19), 30c   *RATING: 61*

Don Tallon
21T 394r (17.13); 50 catches, 8 stumpings   *RATING: 79*

Ray Lindwall
61T 1502r (21.15) 2 100s; 228w (23.03), 26c   *RATING: 93*

Bill Johnston
40T 273r (11.37); 160w (23.91), 16c   *RATING: 86*

Ernie Toshack
12T 73r (14.60) 47w (21.04), 4c   *RATING: 46*

THE CAPTAIN FACTOR   *RATING: 94*

MATCHWINNERS FACTOR   *RATING: 67*

TEAM SCORE: 1008

GODDARD'S 1950 West Indies

Allan Rae ◖◗◖◗
15T 1016r (46.18) 4 100s; 10c *RATING: 58*

Jeff Stollmeyer ◖◗◖◗◖◗◖◗
32T 2159r (42.33) 4 100s; 13w (39.00), 20c *RATING: 69*

Frank Worrell ◖◗◖◗◖◗◖◗◖◗◖◗◖◗◖◗◖◗
51T 3860r (49.48) 9 100s; 69w (38.73), 43c *RATING: 93*

Everton Weekes ◖◗◖◗◖◗◖◗◖◗◖◗◖◗◖◗◖◗
48T 4455r (58.61) 15 100s; 49c *RATING: 92*

Clyde Walcott ◖◗◖◗◖◗◖◗◖◗◖◗◖◗◖◗◖◗
44T 3798r (56.68) 15 100s; 11w (37)) 53c 11st *RATING: 91*

Gerry Gomez ◖◗◖◗
29T 1243r (30.31) 1 100; 58w (27.41), 18c *RATING: 58*

Robert Christiani ◖◗
22T 896r (26.35) 1 100; 3w (36.00), 19c 2st *RATING: 49*

John Goddard ◖◗◖◗
27T 859r (30.67); 33w (31.81) 22c *RATING: 58*

Hines Johnson ◖◗
3T 38r (9.50); 13w (18.30) *RATING: 45*

Sonny Ramadhin ◖◗◖◗◖◗◖◗◖◗◖◗◖◗◖◗
43T 361r (8.20); 158w (28.98), 9c *RATING: 88*

Alf Valentine ◖◗◖◗◖◗◖◗◖◗◖◗◖◗◖◗
36T 141r (4.70) 139w (30.32), 13c *RATING: 87*

THE CAPTAIN FACTOR *RATING: 85*

MATCHWINNERS FACTOR *RATING: 55*

TEAM SCORE: 928

160

HUTTON'S 1953 England

Len Hutton
79T 6971r (56.67) 19 100s; 3 w (77.33) 57c   *RATING: 90*

Bill Edrich
39T 2440r (40.00) 6 100s; 41w (41.29), 39c   *RATING: 76*

Tom Graveney
79T 4882r (44.38) 11 100s; 80c   *RATING: 80*

Denis Compton
78T 5807r (50.06) 17 100s; 25w (56.40) 49c   *RATING: 88*

Willie Watson
23T 879r (25.85) 2100s; 8c   *RATING: 43*

Reg Simpson
27T 1401r (33.35) 4 100s; 2w (11.00), 5c   *RATING: 49*

Trevor Bailey
61T 2290r (29.74) 1 100; 132w (29.21), 32c   *RATING: 80*

Godfrey Evans
91T 2439r (20.49) 2 100s; 173c 46st   *RATING: 82*

Johnny Wardle
28T 653r (19.78); 102w (20.39), 12c   *RATING: 61*

Jim Laker
46T 676r (14.08); 193w (21.24), 12c   *RATING: 87*

Alec Bedser
51T 714r (12.75) 236w (24.89), 26c   *RATING: 88*

THE CAPTAIN FACTOR   *RATING: 91*

MATCHWINNERS FACTOR   *RATING: 65*

TEAM SCORE: 980

161

MAY'S 1956 England

Peter Richardson
34T 2061r (37.47) 5 100s; 6c   *RATING: 53*

Colin Cowdrey
114T 7624r (44.06) 22 100s; 120c   *RATING: 87*

David Sheppard
22T 1172r (37.80) 3 100s; 12c   *RATING: 52*

Peter May
66T 4537r (46.77) 13 100s; 42c   *RATING: 88*

Cyril Washbrook
37T 2569r (42.81) 6 100s; 12c   *RATING: 69*

Trevor Bailey
61T 2290r (29.74) 1 100; 132w (29.21); 32c   *RATING: 80*

Godfrey Evans
91T 2439r (20.49) 2 100s; 173c 46st   *RATING: 82*

Jim Laker
46T 6761r (14.08); 193w (21.24); 12c   *RATING: 88*

Tony Lock
49T 742r (13.74); 174w (25.58); 59c   *RATING: 78*

Fred Trueman
67T 981r (13.81); 307w (21.57); 64c   *RATING: 89*

Brian Statham
70T 675r (11.44); 252w (24.82); 28c   *RATING: 81*

THE CAPTAIN FACTOR   *RATING: 90*

MATCHWINNERS FACTOR   *RATING: 67*

TEAM SCORE: 1004

Colin McDonald
47T 3107r (39.32) 5 100s; 14c

RATING: 66

Bobby Simpson
62T 4869r (46.81) 10 100s; 71w (42.26); 110c   *RATING: 84*

Neil Harvey
79T 6149r (48.42) 21 100s; 3w (40.00); 64c   *RATING: 87*

Norm O'Neill
42T 2779r (45.55) 6 100s; 17w (39.23); 21c   *RATING: 77*

Les Favell
19T 757r (27.03) 1 100; 9c

RATING: 43

Ken Mackay
37T 1507r (33.48); 50w (30.42); 17c   *RATING: 66*

Alan Davidson
44T 1328r (24.59); 186w (20.53); 42c   *RATING: 88*

Richie Benaud
63T 2201r (24.45) 3 100s; 248w (27.03); 65c   *RATING: 90*

Wally Grout
51T 890r (15.08); 163c 24st

RATING: 81

Johnny Martin
8T 214r (17.83); 17w (48.94), 5c   *RATING: 46*

Frank Misson
5T 381r (19.00) 16w (38.50), 6c   *RATING: 41*

THE CAPTAIN FACTOR   *RATING: 97*

MATCHWINNERS FACTOR   *RATING: 56*

TEAM SCORE: 922

Conrad Hunte

44T 32451r (45.06) 8 100s; 2 w (55.00) 16c **RATING: 77**

Joey Carew

19T 1127r (34.15) 1 100; 8w (54.62), 13c **RATING: 50**

Rohan Kanhai

79T 6227r (47.53) 15 100s; 50c **RATING: 84**

Basil Butcher

44T 3104r (43.11) 7 100s; 5w (18.00) 15c **RATING: 73**

Garfield Sobers

93T 8032r (57.78) 26 100s; 235w (34.03); 109c **RATING: 99**

Joe Solomon

27T 1326r (34.00) 1 100; 4w (67.00), 13c **RATING: 45**

Frank Worrell

51T 3860r (49.48) 9 100s; 69w (38.78); 43c **RATING: 93**

Deryck Murray

62T 1993r (22.90); 181c 8st **RATING :81**

Wes Hall

48T 818r (15.73); 192w (26.38); 11c **RATING: 84**

Charlie Griffith

28T 538r (16.56); 94w (28.54) 16c **RATING: 66**

Lance Gibbs

79T 488r (6.97); 309w (29.09), 52c **RATING: 87**

THE CAPTAIN FACTOR **RATING: 92**

MATCHWINNERS FACTOR **RATING: 66**

TEAM SCORE: 996

BACHER'S 1969 South Africa

Barry Richards
4T 508r (72.57) 2 100s; 3c
RATING: 91

Trevor Goddard
41T 2516r (34.46) 1 100; 123w (26.22) 48c
RATING: 82

Ali Bacher
12T 679r (32.33); 10c
RATING: 55

Graeme Pollock
23T 2256r (60.97) 7 100s; 4w (51.00) 17c
RATING: 90

Eddie Barlow
30T 2516r (45.74) 6 100s; 40w (34.05) 35c
RATING: 77

Lee Irvine
4T 353 (50.42) 1 100; 2c
RATING: 64

Dennis Lindsay
19T 1130r (37.66) 3 100s; 57c 2st
RATING: 72

Herbert Lance
13T 591r (28.14); 12w (39.91); 7c
RATING: 45

Mike Procter
7T 226r (25.11); 41w (15.02), 4c
RATING: 89

Peter Pollock
28T 607r (21.67); 116w (24.18), 9c
RATING: 78

John Traicos
3T 8r (4.00); 4w (51.75), 4c
RATING: 40

THE CAPTAIN FACTOR   *RATING: 86*

MATCHWINNERS FACTOR   *RATING: 57*

TEAM SCORE: 926

CHAPPELL'S 1975 Australia

Ian Redpath
66T 4737r (43.45) 8 100s; 83c   *RATING: 76*

Rick McCosker
25T 1622r (39.56) 4100s; 210c   *RATING: 60*

Greg Chappell
87T 6110r (53.86) 24 100s; 47w (40.70), 122c   *RATING: 92*

Ian Chappell
75T 5345r (42.42) 14 100s; 32w (43.71) 105c   *RATING: 84*

Ross Edwards
20T 1171r (40.37) 2 100s; 7c   *RATING: 51*

Doug Walters
74T 5357r (48.26) 15 100s; 49w (29.08), 43c   *RATING: 84*

Rodney Marsh
96T 3633r (26.51) 3 100s; 343c 12st   *RATING: 86*

Max Walker
34T 586r (19.53); 138w (27.47); 12c   *RATING: 68*

Dennis Lillee
70T 905r (13,71); 355w (23.92); 23c   *RATING: 95*

Ashley Mallett
38T 430r (11.62); 132w (29.84), 30c   *RATING:63*

Jeff Thomson
51T 641r (12.09) 200w (27.03), 19c   *RATING: 83*

THE CAPTAIN FACTOR   *RATING: 95*

MATCHWINNERS FACTOR   *RATING: 66*

TEAM SCORE: 1003

BREARLEY'S 1981 England

Geoff Boycott
108T 8114r (47.72) 22 100s; 7 w (54.57) 33c **RATING: 89**

Graham Gooch
59T 3746r (37.08) 7 100s; 13w (42.00); 57c **RATING: 67**

David Gower
96T 6789r (44.66) 14 100s; 66c **RATING: 83**

Mike Brearley
39T 1442r (22.88); 52c **RATING: 47**

Mike Gatting
58T 3563r (40.95) 9 100s; 49c **RATING: 69**

Peter Willey
26T 1184r (26.90) 2 100s; 7w (65.14); 3c **RATING: 43**

Ian Botham
94T 5057r (34.87) 14 100s; 373w (27.86); 109c **RATING: 97**

John Emburey
46T 1027r (19.01); 115w (33.52); 28c **RATING :62**

Bob Taylor
57T 1156r (16.28); 167c 7st **RATING: 67**

Graham Dilley
30T 391r (13.48); 99w (30.02) 9c **RATING: 64**

Bob Willis
90T 840r (11.50); 325w (25.20), 39c **RATING: 82**

THE CAPTAIN FACTOR **RATING: 96**

MATCHWINNERS FACTOR **RATING: 52**

TEAM SCORE: 918

167

Gordon Greenidge
74T 5165r (47.38) 12 100s; 68c   *RATING: 88*

Desmond Haynes
62T 3852r (42.32) 8 100s; 39c   *RATING: 70*

Larry Gomes
57T 3099r (40.77) 9 100s; 17c   *RATING: 67*

Viv Richards
85T 6395r (53.73) 20 100s; 20w (53.03) 17c   *RATING: 93*

Clive Lloyd
110T 7515r (46.67) 19 100s; 10w (62.20); 85c   *RATING: 90*

Jeff Dujon
40T 1876 (38.28) 4 100s; 130c 3st   *RATING: 69*

Malcolm Marshall
48T 985r (18.58); 231w (21.23); 23c   *RATING: 88*

Eldine Baptiste
9T 224r (24.88); 15w (32.40); 2c   *RATING: 51*

Roger Harper
19T 352r (16.00); 40w (27.25), 24c   *RATING: 59*

Michael Holding
59T 901r (14.00); 249w (23.28); 21c   *RATING: 88*

Joel Garner
56T 661r (12.96); 247w (21.16), 39c   *RATING: 89*

THE CAPTAIN FACTOR   *RATING: 93*

MATCHWINNERS FACTOR   *RATING: 69*

TEAM SCORE: 1014

THE TEAMS

1: Clive Lloyd's 1984 West Indies
2: Don Bradman's 1948 Australia
3: Peter May's 1956 England
4: Ian Chappell's 1975 Australia
5: Frank Worrell's 1963 West Indies
6: Len Hutton's 1953 England
7: John Goddard's 1950 West Indies
8: Ali Bacher's 1969 South Africa
9: Richie Benaud's 1961 Australia
10: Mike Brearley's 1981 England

THE CAPTAINS

1: Richie Benaud (Australia)
2: Mike Brearley (England)
3: Ian Chappell (Australia)
4: Don Bradman (Australia)
5: Clive Lloyd (West Indies)
6: Frank Worrell (West Indies)
7: Len Hutton (England)
8: Peter May (England)
9: Ali Bacher (South Africa)
10: John Goddard (West Indies)

169

TOM GRAVENEY'S FINAL ASSESSMENT

Sorry, but I think the computer has got it wrong! I prefer to deal in flesh and blood feelings rather than cold facts and figures, and I have no doubt at all that despite what the statistics might allegedly prove **there has not been a better team in my lifetime than Don Bradman's Australian tourists of 1948.**

Maybe I'm old fashioned, but I am very suspicious and sceptical about the use of computers as a barometer of who has done what in sport. You cannot program a computer to know, for instance, how a batsman feels when waiting for a thunderbolt from a Lindwall or a Lillee, or what it's like for a bowler to be faced by a Bradman or a Viv Richards in full flow. The computer may be able to work things out on paper, but out on the pitch where it really matters it's the human factor that counts. After careful consideration of all the players and personalities involved, I have to say that nothing will convince me that there has been a better all-round team than the Bradman side that outplayed a top-quality England squad led by Norman Yardley.

Clive Lloyd's West Indies side was a real mean machine, but I feel a vital contributory factor in their success was the point that many modern batsmen have not mastered the correct technique to deal with really quick bowling. Because of the glut of one-day run-scrambling cricket, they pick up bad habits that they take into the Test arena with them. They invariably fail to get right behind the line of the ball and play straight. I can assure you that all the batsmen in Bradman's 1948 team had come through a tough school that demanded textbook technique, and I know the West Indies four-pronged pace attack would not have skittled them as they did David Gower's England in the two successive 'blackwash' series.

I have tried to imagine a series between Bradman's team of 1948 and Clive Lloyd's side of 1984, and in my heart of hearts I *know* that the Aussies would have come out on top. They had superior all-round batting strength. For instance, Ray Lindwall coming in at number nine would have been accomplished enough with the bat to have batted six or seven in most other sides. I notice that the majestic left-hander Neil Harvey was left out of the team by the computer because Sam Loxton played three Tests to his two on the 1948 tour. The computer is brainless! There *must* be a place for Harvey in the team. He scored a century in his Test debut on the 1948 tour and was never out of the side for the following 14 years. I am positive that the likes of Sidney

Barnes, Arthur Morris, the supreme Bradman, Lindsay Hassett, Miller and Harvey would have been able to compile runs against the West Indies pace men, but I am not so sure that the West Indies could have coped with the combination of speed and cunning from Lindwall and Miller. Ray Lindwall was not just about blinding speed. He was the thinking man's fast bowler, and could make the ball dip and swerve and move both ways. As for Keith Miller, he was so unpredictable that not only the batsmen but even Keith himself was not sure what his next delivery would do. I've seen him bowl a bouncer, a leg cutter, a slow off-break and a yorker all in the space of one over and each ball could have got a wicket. When he was really letting loose, Keith could be as quick as any bowler in the history of the game.

A lot has been made of the fact that Clive Lloyd's West Indies played with a battery of four fast bowlers and that there was no respite for the batsmen. Let us not forget that Bradman was able to bring Bill Johnston on as first-change bowler, and I promise you that he could be extremely sharp with express left-arm deliveries that would buck and rear on any pitch offering him the slightest encouragement. Ernie Toshack was not in the same league of speed as the West Indians, but I have rarely seen a medium-fast bowler to match him for nagging accuracy. He could tie the most prolific batsmen down by dropping just short of a length on the leg side and making it almost impossible to get the ball away. Ian Johnson was, without question, a superior spinner to Roger Harper even if there was the suspicion of a throwing action when he delivered his quicker ball.

On the batting front, Clive Lloyd's West Indies had in Gordon Greenidge, Viv Richards and Clive himself three undoubted 'all-time great' masters. But their three other front-line batsmen, Desmond Haynes, Larry Gomes and Jeff Dujon, were all inclined to periods of inconsistency that would have been quickly exploited by Lindwall and Miller. Their tail started very early, with Malcolm Marshall coming in at number seven. Don Tallon was unarguably a better wicket keeper than Dujon, but was not as impressive with the bat.

So after weighing all things up, my verdict has to be that Bradman's team would emerge as the winners, with Clive Lloyd's side beaten but not disgraced.

I have several other quarrels with the computer. I think it has given Peter May's 1956 team far too high a rating. If it had not been for the spinning genius of Jim Laker and a couple of, let's say, dodgy wickets, the Ashes that year might easily have been won by Ian Johnson's Aussies. In my personal view, Len Hutton's 1953 England team was a stronger and better balanced side than the May team. The selectors finally got it right for the last Test of the series in which England clinched the Ashes for the first time in 19 years. The team that won at The Oval was the finest I had the privilege of playing with during my England career. Just let me remind you of the line-up:

Len Hutton, Bill Edrich, Peter May, Denis Compton, myself, Trevor Bailey, Godfrey Evans, Jim Laker, Tony Lock, Fred Trueman, Alec Bedser.

I doubt in all modesty whether there has been a finer side representing England in post-war cricket.

It is beyond my comprehension how the computer could have rated May's side – for whom I managed to play two games – above Ian Chappell's 1975 Australians and Frank Worrell's 1963 West Indies. Lillee and Thomson gave the Chappell team such pace and purpose that they could almost have challenged for the No. 1 position, and the fearsome combination of Wes Hall and Charlie Griffith put Worrell's West Indies very high in my estimation.

This is how my final top ten table reads:

1: Don Bradman's 1948 Australia
2: Clive Lloyd's 1984 West Indies
3: Ian Chappell's 1975 Australia
4: Frank Worrell's 1963 West Indies
5: Len Hutton's 1953 England
6: Peter May's 1956 England
7: Ali Bacher's 1969 South Africa
8: John Goddard's 1950 West Indies
9: Richie Benaud's 1961 Australia
10: Mike Brearley's 1981 England

You will see that I have rated Ali Bacher's 1969 South Africans one place higher than the computer. Had it not been for their isolation because of the poison of politics, I believe they would have been much higher up the table. There have been few sides able to boast a match-winning trio of the class of Barry Richards, Graeme Pollock and Mike Procter. They can be mentioned in the same breath as the wonderful 'three Ws' – Worrell, Weekes and Walcott – of the 1950 West Indies team. It was John Goddard's side that gave me the biggest headache when trying to decide

172

where to place them. I finally dropped them down to eighth position because they were so weak in the new-ball bowling department. Ramadhin and Valentine were exceptional spinners of the ball, but they could not frighten and intimidate batsmen like the super-fast pacemen. They could baffle and bewilder them, but not scare them into making mistakes. It's that fear factor that the computer was unable to take into account.

Lovers of the modern game might well want to take me to task for putting Mike Brearley's 1981 England team 10th and last in the list. My feelings about that side are the same as about the Peter May team. Jim Laker was the one major difference between the two teams in 1956, and Ian Botham held the balance of power in 1981. But for Botham's astonishing contribution there is little doubt that Kim Hughes's Australians would have won the Ashes.

Well, that's my final *Top Teams* assessment. We hope we have given you plenty to think and argue about. If nothing else I've found it a good exercise in nostalgia, and I stand by my judgment that Don Bradman's 1948 Australians—the side that was dominant in my first season as a full-time cricketer—was the greatest of them all. Which side would **YOU** choose?

We have taken the 11 specialist players with the highest computer ratings and put them together in a 'dream team' combination and have added Tom Graveney's personal assessment of each player. Rodney Marsh was the highest-rated wicket keeper, but we have selected that West Indian powerhouse Clyde Walcott because of his batting strength:

LEN HUTTON (England)

A master opener, Len would face any new-ball attack with confidence and that dogged determination of his that would break the hearts of bowlers trying to find a way through his stonewall defence. He had the defensive technique to tame even the most hostile bowlers. Len would give this 'dream team' the strongest possible foundation.

BARRY RICHARDS (South Africa)

The ideal partner for Hutton. While Len would have cemented himself in before going for the runs, Barry would have attacked from the first ball he received. His aggression and natural desire to get on with the business of scoring runs would have provided the perfect balance to Hutton's cautious approach. As far as Barry was concerned, *any* ball was there to be hit.

DON BRADMAN (Australia)

The sight of The Don coming down the pavilion steps to join either Hutton or Barry Richards for the second wicket would have brought despair to the hearts of the most willing bowlers. There has never been anybody to touch Bradman as a dictator of attacks, as is proved beyond all argument by his remarkable Test average of 99.94.

174

VIV RICHARDS (West Indies)

It would be the nearest you could get to a cricketers' paradise to see Viv Richards and Don Bradman together at the wicket – that is unless you are the bowler unlucky enough to have to bowl to them! Viv goes his own way as a batsman, but for all his invention and flair never forgets the basic technique of getting behind the line of the ball.

CLYDE WALCOTT (West Indies)

I would put Walcott just about equal with those other members of the 'three Ws' trio – Worrell and Weekes – as a batting force, but he justifies his selection in this 'dream team' because of his ability to play behind the stumps. He was such a big man that he lacked real agility as a wicket keeper, but his runs contribution would more than make up for any lapses with the gloves.

GARY SOBERS (West Indies)

Without doubt, the greatest cricketer of my lifetime. With his majestic batting and three variations of bowling, he would be the key man even in this star-studded side. Apart from all that he achieved with the bat and the ball, Gary – when at the peak of his fitness – was also one of the finest of all close fielders whose tremendous reflexes meant that any catchable ball was sure to be snapped up.

IAN BOTHAM (England)

As a player who has carried England on his back for so many matches, it would be fascinating to see how Botham would react to playing as 'just another' member of the team. I have a feeling that he is at his best in a crisis, but that is a situation he would be unlikely to experience when coming in at number seven in this 'dream team.'

KEITH MILLER (Australia)

Any side that could afford the luxury of having the swash-buckling Keith Miller coming to the wicket at number eight would be worth walking a million miles to see. With Lindwall and Lillee in the firing-line, he would not even have the responsibility of taking the new ball. Fancy being able to call on Miller and Botham as your change bowlers!

RICHIE BENAUD (Australia)

As well as for his exceptional ability as a leg spinner, Richie makes it into this team for his qualities as a captain. I know that he would consider himself in Heaven if he could toss the new ball to Lindwall and Lillee, with Miller, Botham and Sobers in reserve. And imagine being able to say to the likes of Bradman and Viv Richards: "Just play it naturally, chaps, and let the runs come. We'll be looking for a declaration around about tea-time tomorrow."

RAY LINDWALL (Australia)

The king of the fast bowlers. I'm sure his bat would not be needed, but if it were he would be capable of scoring a quick half century. But it is his bowling that wins him his place. He would unsettle the finest batsmen with balls that would not only be delivered at high speed but also with movement either way off the pitch that would make them desperately difficult to play.

DENNIS LILLEE (Australia)

I cannot think of a more fearsome twosome than Lindwall and Lillee. They would make a deadly combination, and if there were any batsmen in the galaxy who could survive their onslaught with the new ball they would then have the doubtful privilege of facing Keith Miller and Ian Botham. Oh yes, and Gary Sobers is just warming up for his spell!

Our 'dream team' needs a 'dream match' and we have come up with this side to oppose them in an imaginary five-day Test at Lord's:

Geoff Boycott (England), Gordon Greenidge (West Indies), Greg Chappell (Australia), Denis Compton (England), Graeme Pollock (South Africa), Frank Worrell (West Indies, capt.), Rodney Marsh (Australia), Jim Laker (England), Fred Trueman (England), Michael Holding (West Indies), Joel Garner (West Indies).

Now it's YOUR turn to play the selecting game. Which team will YOU choose?